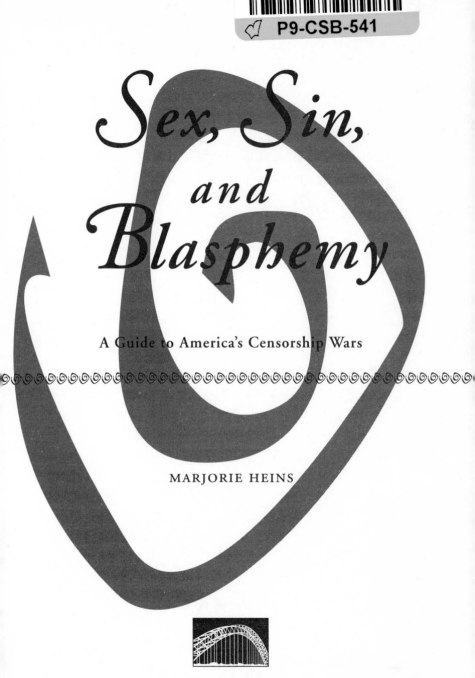

Sex, Sin, and Blasphemy

A Guide to America's Censorship Wars

MARJORIE HEINS

THE NEW PRESS
New York

Published in the United States by The New Press, New York
Distributed by W. W. Norton & Company, Inc.
500 Fifth Avenue, New York, NY 10110

LIBRARY OF CONGRESS CATALOGING-IN-PUBLICATION DATA
Heins, Marjorie.

Sex, sin, and blasphemy : a guide to America's censorship

wars / by Marjorie Heins. – 1st ed.

p.   cm.

Includes bibliographical references.

ISBN 1-56584-062-3 – ISBN 1-56584-048-8 (pbk.)

1. Censorship–United States. 2. Sex in art. I. Title.

Z658.U5H43   1993

363.3'1'0973—dc20   92-50837

Book design by Laura Lindgren

The New Press was established in 1990 as a not-for-profit
alternative to the large, commercial publishing houses
currently dominating the book publishing industry. The
New Press operates in the public interest rather than for
private gain, and is committed to publishing, in innovative
ways, works of educational, cultural, and community value,
that are often deemed insufficiently profitable.

The New Press's editorial offices are located at
the City University of New York.

www.thenewpress.com

9 8 7 6 5 4 3 2

CONTENTS

Congress shall make no law respecting an establishment of religion, or prohibiting the free exercise thereof; or abridging the freedom of speech or of the press; or the right of the people peaceably to assemble and to petition the Government for a redress of grievances.

—U.S. Constitution, First Amendment

ACKNOWLEDGEMENTS

This book is a product of nearly two years of front-line experiences in the censorship wars it describes. It wouldn't have been possible without the help and support of numerous people and institutions, foremost among them the American Civil Liberties Union, which created an Arts Censorship Project in 1991 and hired me to direct it. I feel privileged to have been given that opportunity to contribute to the defense of First Amendment freedoms in perilous times.

Thanks are due the ACLU's Executive Director, Ira Glasser, and its Legal Director, john powell, for affording me the opportunity to learn about what's going on in the censorship wars and try to figure out ways to be part of the solution. Others at the ACLU, particularly Steven Shapiro, Loren Siegel, Phil Gutis, Bob Peck, Diane Weiss, Bill Rubenstein, Ruth Harlow, Isabelle Katz Pinzler, and our magnificent president, Nadine Strossen, have helped to educate me about First Amendment issues. Thanks also for their tremendous work to the staff of the Arts Censorship Project in 1992, Jon Cummings and Kenia Olivera.

The Nathan Cummings Foundation, which provided the seed money to start the Arts Censorship Project, and especially Charles Halperin and Joan Shigekawa, should also be thanked for their prescience and their concern for artistic freedom. Other important sources of support, both moral and financial, have been the Robert Sterling Clark Foundation, and especially its Executive Director, Margaret Ayers; Rob Tannenbaum of the Nathan Tannenbaum Foundation; Archibald Gillies and Emily Todd of the Andy Warhol Foundation; playwright David Henry Hwang and the other members of the Arts Censorship Project's advisory board, and of course The New Press, which liked the idea of a guide to arts censorship, and especially New Press founder André Schiffrin and my perspicacious editor, David Sternbach.

One of the special pleasures of my ongoing work against censorship have been the fascinating people I have met who are laboring in the same vineyards. Their dedication is outstanding, and I have learned much from their knowledge of the arts, politics, law, and the interactions among the three. They include David Mendoza of the National Campaign for Freedom of Expression; Charlotte Murphy and Helen Brunner of the National Association of Artists' Organizations; Chris Finan of the Media Coalition; Gara LaMarche of the Fund for Free Expression; Leanne Katz of the National Coalition Against Censorship; Siobhan Dowd of the PEN Freedom to Write Committee; Judy Krug of the American Library Association; Gail Markels of the Motion Picture Association of America; Marcia Pally, feminist scholar and cofounder of Feminists for Free Expression; and others, too numerous to mention, who are struggling for artistic freedom in these difficult times.

Perhaps most amazing to me are the hard-working people at ACLU affiliates around the country. When I first came to the ACLU in 1982, I could not have found two more congenial, dedicated, good-humored, bosses than John Roberts, Executive Director of the Civil Liberties Union of Massachusetts, and John Reinstein, its Legal Director. They taught me a great deal about how to survive emotionally and physically while doing civil liberties work year after year.

Other outstanding affiliate staffers who have helped me and the Arts Censorship Project enormously include Ann Brick at the ACLU of Northern California, Alan Parachini and Carol Sobel at the Southern California affiliate, Doug Honig and Kathleen Taylor in Washington State, Janet Arenz in Oregon, Art Spitzer in the District of Columbia, Harvey Grossman and Jane Whicher of the ACLU of Illinois, Hedy Weinberg in Tennessee, Joe Cook in Texas, Gerry Weber in Georgia, Robyn Blumner and Nina Vinik in Florida, Shirley Pedler in Louisiana, Deborah Gilman and Bill Roath in Minnesota, Jack Van Valkenburgh in Idaho, Art Eisenberg and Pam Katz in New York, Jim Shields and William Simpson in North Carolina, Stu Comstock-Gay and Susan Goering in Maryland, Dick Kurtenbach and Carla Dugger in Kansas/Western Missouri, Bill Schatz in Nebraska, Howard Simon in Michigan, David Miller in Colorado, Deborah Leavey and Stefan Presser in Pennsylvania, and Judith Mellen in Delaware. If I've left anybody out, I apologize, for as everybody at the ACLU knows, our state affiliates are the crucial front-line defenders of free speech and individual rights.

As important to the defense of First Amendment freedoms as ACLU staffers are, the job could not be done without the many private attorneys who generously volunteer their services to ACLU clients in legal cases. Grappling with arts censorship incidents all across the country, I've had the good fortune to meet and work with attorneys who care deeply about individual dignity and liberty, and who are willing to make sacrifices to defend them.

I've learned much from these ACLU cooperating attorneys, as well as from our talented corps of staff lawyers, and from brilliant First Amendment advocates like David Cole, Nan Hunter, Mary Dorman, and Ellen Yaroshefsky, my co-counsel in the "NEA 4" case (see Chapter 6).

Most of all, I've learned from the artists, in all media, whose pioneering, challenging, uncompromising work has generated many of the censorship controversies you'll be reading about in the pages that follow. "Artists are society's watchers, critics, and champions. They speak the unspeakable, even if it manifests itself in horrifying, untidy, or esoteric matters."[1] It is to them that I dedicate this book.

All errors and faults in this volume of course are my own. The ACLU and the others who have helped make it possible are responsible only for its virtues.

NINETEEN HUNDRED AND NINETY EIGHT IS AN OPPORTUNE time for me to be introducing a second printing of *Sex, Sin, and Blasphemy*. The book was originally published in 1993, two years after I had come to the national office of the American Civil Liberties Union to begin its Arts Censorship Project. Now, after five more years and many more censorship battles, I have just left the ACLU. These years have given me not only invaluable opportunities to participate in historic free-expression cases but also an enhanced appreciation of the depth and intractability of the human impulse to censor.

In these past five years, for example, efforts to control "indecent" speech in the explosive new medium of cyberspace have been unrelenting, despite the Supreme Court's 1997 ruling in *Reno v. ACLU* that the online medium is entitled to the same high level of First Amendment protection as newspapers, films, and books. The commonly asserted, though rarely questioned, justification for these censorship initiatives—the need to protect minors—has also driven the expansion of ratings systems, from movies and music recordings (see chapter 2) to television and computers. Meanwhile, young people are losing free-speech protection in their schools, as courts more frequently defer to local officials' censorship of curricular and library materials. The Supreme Court's June 1998 decision in *National Endowment for the Arts v. Finley* perhaps summed up these highly political five years in the "censorship wars" by ruling that the "decency and respect" standard inserted by Congress into the National Endowment for the Arts' decision-making process (see chapter 6) does not violate the First Amendment.

Despite these developments, neither the terms of the censorship debate nor the dynamics of censorship have really changed. Many incidents described in *Sex, Sin, and Blasphemy* occurred in the early 1990s, but they have been replicated countless times in the ensuing years, with changes only in the name of the book, film or entertainer, and the location of the controversy. The basic pattern persists: accusations that some work of art of entertainment contains immoral, blasphemous, or other presumably bad ideas, followed by demands for removal, restriction, silencing, or suppression.

"Indecency in Cyberspace"

In 1995, when the various bills that eventually became the 1996 Communications Decency Act (the "CDA") were in legislative gestation, many of us at the ACLU were still struggling to learn elementary computer operations. Only the most electronically sophisticated among us were surfing the World Wide Web, and the web itself was more a participatory, communitarian network of newsgroups and chatrooms than the commercialized "information supermarket" that it was soon to become. Within that participatory network, however, there was plenty of sex talk, an increasing number of pornographic online sites, and a brisk trade in sexual images. Panic over all this online sex, combined with puzzlement about the new technology, drove the legislative proposals that culminated in the CDA.

Congress chose for this first legislative foray into cyberspace a legal standard of "indecency" that the Supreme Court had approved in its famous 1978 decision upholding the Federal Communications Commission's regulation of radio and television broadcasting (*FCC v. Pacifica Foundation*; see chapter 1). This "indecency" standard differed from the Court's test for identifying criminally punishable "obscenity" in at least two important respects. First, "indecent" speech, unlike "obscenity," did not have to be "lascivious" or appeal to "prurient interests" to be regulated; it needed only be "patently offensive," according to "contemporary community standards," whatever those might be. Second, again unlike obscenity, which the Supreme Court had said lacks First Amendment protection, "indecent" speech can have "serious literary, artistic, political, or scientific value," yet still be regulated in the interest of protecting, or guiding the moral development of, the young. This meant that all manner of valuable literary, artistic, and otherwise educational material was potentially indecent, as long as the subject was sex–or, for that matter, even vulgar words.

Indeed, in the *Pacifica* case itself, the Supreme Court approved sanctions against a radio station that broadcast George Carlin's satiric "Filthy Words" monologue, not for sexual purposes but simply to make a political comment on society's linguistic taboos. A majority of the justices in *Pacifica* assumed, without explanation, that hearing these words would be harmful to kids. The entire monologue, in all its sidesplitting hilarity, was reproduced as an appendix to the *Pacifica* decision. Because the monologue had been officially judged indecent, any Internet sites containing the appendix to *Pacifica* could be guilty of violating the 1996 CDA.

This was only the most ironic of many examples of how the CDA infringed the First Amendment rights of adults and, we argued, older minors as well. Two of my favorite illustrations, from the *ACLU v. Reno* trial in Philadelphia in the spring of 1996, came from the government's expert witnesses, in response to questions from the three judges who heard the case. The first question was whether the famous *Vanity Fair* cover photograph of a naked, pregnant Demi Moore would be "patently offensive" and therefore indecent, according to the community standards of, say, rural Minnesota. The expert, a federal law enforcement officer who specialized in computer pornography, said that it could well be, because the photo was for entertainment rather than educational purposes. A different expert witness responded affirmatively when asked whether a vulgar comment such as "Fuck the CDA," in an online chatroom would be indecent.

The CDA, of course, only criminalized this "patently offensive" or indecent online speech if it was "displayed in a manner available to" people under 18. But because minors traveling through cyberspace are generally indistinguishable from adults, the CDA essentially banned such speech entirely. Congress had tried to address this problem by writing defenses into the law for good-faith efforts to identify and screen out minors from indecent or patently offensive communications. But existing screening technologies were crude and ineffective, and their cost would have been prohibitive for most of the nonprofit organizations that joined in the _Reno_ lawsuit. In addition, many of these organizations _wanted_ to communicate on sexual subjects to young people–among them the ACLU (which hosted an online teen chat about masturbation), Human Rights Watch (which offered news stories about torture and rape), Planned Parenthood, the Safer Sex Web Page, and the Critical Path AIDS Project (all of which provided explicit discussions of contraception and safer sex), and the Wildcat Press (which published an online magazine for gay and lesbian teens).

It was a crucial part of the ACLU legal strategy in _Reno_ to introduce evidence of the valuable, nonharmful character of much online communication about sex, nudity, and even vulgar words that could be considered patently offensive and therefore illegal under the CDA. This strategy was designed to focus the courts, including ultimately the Supreme Court, on actually analyzing, perhaps even reconsidering, past judicial statements about the government's "compelling need" to protect kids from "patently offensive" speech.

Thus, in addition to examples suggested by the trial judges themselves (erotic Hindu sculptures and Henry Miller's *Tropic of Cancer* were mentioned along with *Vanity Fair*), we presented evidence describing explicit online sex and reproductive information; literature and art with sexual themes; and discussions about homosexuality, feminism, rape, and censorship.

The June 1997 Supreme Court decision in *Reno v. ACLU* noted this evidence, adding to it the example of e-mail exchanges on sexual topics between parents and teenagers. The prospect of parents being made into criminals by the CDA was a powerful argument for the justices that the law was hopelessly overbroad. The Supreme Court decision also affirmed the Philadelphia judges' findings that the CDA's defenses were ineffective, thus rendering the law an unconstitutional infringement on the First Amendment rights of adults. Although the *Reno* decision twice repeated the mantra that at least some patently offensive speech about sex is harmful to minors, the Court did not identify what sexual communications might fit in that category. By contrast, Justice John Paul Stevens's opinion for the Court devoted a long section to explaining why the indecency standard was too vague for anyone really to know what it meant, and to tailor her communications accordingly. The Court rejected the Justice Department's arguments that cyberspace should enjoy less First Amendment protection than books, magazines, or movies, and instead spoke in glowing terms of the tremendous potential of "this new marketplace of ideas"–the "'most participatory form of mass speech yet developed,'" with content "'as diverse as human thought.'"[1]

Despite these stirring words, the proverbial ink was barely dry on the *Reno* opinion when political players from the White House to the "Enough is Enough" antipornography campaign to industry giants such as America Online began to float alternative proposals for controlling speech in cyberspace. A bill sponsored by Senator Dan Coats was a narrower version of the CDA, imposing a "harmful to minors" or "obscenity lite" rather than an "indecency" test (see chapter 1), and regulating only websites engaged in commercial activity. In October 1998, Congress passed the Coats bill, and the ACLU once again filed suit, with plaintiffs including Androgyny Books, Inc., Obgyn.net, Powell's Bookstore, and the online magazine, *Salon.*

Other legislative initiatives focused on the wide variety of Internet rating and filtering programs that were by now flooding the market. A bill authored by Senator John McCain in 1998 required that any public school or library receiving federal aid for Internet connections must install software that rates and blocks purportedly inappropriate online sites. Rating and blocking software, however, is an extremely crude tool for controlling minors' access to cyberspace. It filters out large amounts of valuable, educational material. This is because the software must rely either on "keyword" identification or on subjective human judgment about the relative offensiveness or controversiality of online speech. (Most products rely on both methods.) The keyword system cannot distinguish between the use of terms such as "sex" or "breast" in pornography and in literature or medical information, thus blocking Internet sites that mention "Middlesex" County, "Anne Sexton," or "breast cancer." The subjective approach is equally problematic: it uses squads of individual screeners to make inevitably hasty, discretionary decisions about whether to label hundreds of thousands of Internet sites based on slippery, intangible categories of disapproved subject matter. Some software programs even block any online speech critical of their manufacturer.[2]

As 1998 draws to an end, the battle over free speech in cyberspace is clearly far from over.

Ratings Redux: Television and the V-Chip

Rating and blocking schemes, of course, were not a new idea when they began to be adopted for the Internet. First in movies, then by the late 1980s in music recordings, the entertainment industry developed ratings in hopes of discouraging government regulation (see chapters 2 and 4). In 1996, ratings finally came to television.

The so-called v-chip law was a part of the same omnibus 1996 CDA that led to the *Reno v. ACLU* case. (Only the provisions of the CDA relating to indecency on the Internet were challenged in *Reno*.) The v-chip provisions forced the television industry to create a ratings system by mandating that after February 1998 all TV sets with screens 13 inches or larger must be equipped with a device able to read electronic ratings of shows, and block those shows to which certain ratings are attached. The ratings themselves were to be developed "voluntarily" by the television industry and approved by the FCC. The law mandated that if the industry did not "voluntarily" create a satisfactory ratings scheme, then the FCC must "prescribe" one. As critics ruefully observed, this law gave new meaning to the word "voluntary."

Congress did not leave it to the TV industry to decide what types of programming must be rated. Both the legislative "findings" section of the v-chip law and it substantive provisions singled out violent, sexual, "or other indecent material" as the subject matter that must be labeled and thereby subject to blocking. Neither Congress not the industry group that subsequently created the TV ratings made any effort to contextualize the labels—to distinguish, for example, documentaries about human rights abuse or films such as *Amistad* or *Schindler's List* from gratuitous violence in action movies, or shows featuring plotless, gyrating body parts. Nor was there any serious discussion of whether violent, sexual, or other "indecent" content was necessarily harmful to minors. Contrary to Congress's announced "findings" in the v-chip law, social science studies on media violence have not established that it has any significant effect on behavior—nor could social science produce such proof, given the inevitably arbitrary conditions of laboratory studies, the either small or non-existent statistical correlations that tend to be found, and the elastic and variable definitions of both media violence and human aggression that different researchers have used.

The television industry responded to the v-chip law initially by announcing its resistance to "voluntary" labeling. But it soon capitulated, and after several months' work unveiled an age-based rating scheme that it invited all television channels to adopt, but that gave no actual information about program content. In response to widespread criticism that a labeling system without information about program content was useless, the industry group revised its plan so that it incorporated both age- and content-based ratings. The content categories were "V" for violence, "S" for sex, "D" for suggestive dialogue, and "L" for coarse language. Only two of the major networks, NBC and BET, refused to adopt the content-specific ratings.

It will probably take years to determine the effects of television ratings. Some producers and scriptwriters understandably fear that networks will pressure them to eschew controversial content in order to avoid ratings that are likely to repel advertisers or reduce audience size. Of course, much the same dynamic has existed historically in the television industry, through internal standards departments. The diversity and frankness that arrived on television screens with the advent of cable was to a large extent a departure from the decades of self-censorship that kept television relatively bland and noncontroversial through most of its history. How much diversity and frankness survives the v-chip remains to be seen.

Harm to Minors

As the CDA and TV ratings sagas suggest, the issue that largely dominated censorship spin-doctoring in the mid-1990s was "harm to minors."[3] As political rhetoric about protecting women from pornography (see chapter 7) lost some of its intensity, protecting children became a more palatable and less easily disputable substitute. It also united a wide range of disparate interests: conservatives campaigning to keep explicit sexual information and ideas from children and teens; liberals concerned about the effects of TV violence; child protection advocates who believe that sex or violence in the media is causally related to bad behavior. It was difficult in these heated circumstances to make a politically palatable argument that teenagers, even younger minors, do have First Amendment rights, including rights to view violent, sexual, or other controversial expression.

As a matter of constitutional law, First Amendment protection for minors goes back at least to the landmark 1969 Supreme Court decision, *Tinker v. Des Moines Independent School District.* Sometimes known as the "black armband" case, *Tinker* involved public school students who were punished when they refused administrators' orders to remove armbands they had worn to school to protest the Vietnam War. In affirming the students' right to express their political views while at school in this symbolic, nondisruptive way, the Supreme Court announced that neither teachers nor students "shed their constitutional rights to freedom of speech or expression at the schoolhouse gate," and that schoolchildren are not simply "closed circuit recipients of only that which the State chooses to communicate."[4]

Four justices expressed much the same sentiment 13 years later in a case involving the removal of books by Kurt Vonnegut,

Langston Hughes, and Richard Wright, among others, from a public high school library in response to school board objections that the works were "anti-American, anti-Christian, anti-Semitic, and just plain filthy."[5] An opinion by Justice William Brennan explained that a "school library, no less than any other public library, is a place dedicated to quiet, to knowledge, and to beauty. ... Students must always remain free to inquire, to study and to evaluate, to gain new maturity and understanding."[6] School boards may not remove books from libraries for "narrowly partisan or political" reasons; "our Constitution does not permit the official suppression of _ideas_."[7]

But the justices in the library case also acknowledged that public schools have an ideological role in inculcating civic values, and wide discretion to fashion educational policies. In later Supreme Court decisions, this "inculcation of values" factor has consistently trumped students' free-speech claims. Thus, the justices ruled in 1986 that administrators could discipline a student for making a sophomoric, sexually suggestive speech at a school assembly, and two years later they upheld a principal's authority to censor articles on divorce and teen pregnancy from a student newspaper.[8]

Lower courts got the message, and by the late 1990s were permitting school officials very broad leeway, even where their decisions were pedagogically dubious or clearly driven by ideological agendas. In 1998, for example, a federal appeals court reversed a jury verdict in favor of a Missouri teacher who had been fired for allowing her creative writing students to read aloud their own works containing profane or vulgar language. The court explained that a school board has "a legitimate academic interest in prohibiting profanity by students in their creative writing," because such a ban teaches them "generally acceptable social standards."[9] What seemed missing from this court decision was any appreciation of the nature and function of creative writing, of the real-world ways in which adolescents express themselves, or of the extent to which some of the greatest literature uses profane or vulgar words.

An even more troubling appellate court decision in 1998 approved the demotion of a highly successful drama teacher who had coached her advanced acting class in an award-winning performance of a play that addressed themes of divorce, homosexuality, and unwed pregnancy. The demotion resulted from a complaint by one parent to the school principal about the content of the play. The most remarkable aspect of the majority opinion in this case was its reliance on Plato's *Republic* as authority for censoring the literature available to young people. In the passage quoted, Plato writes that

> a young person cannot judge what is allegorical and what is literal; anything that he receives into his mind at that age is likely to become indelible and unalterable; and therefore it is most important that the tales which the young first hear should be models of virtuous thoughts.[10]

Even putting aside the fact that high school drama students are capable of distinguishing the "allegorical" from the "literal," Plato's ideal republic was a totalitarian state in which art and ideas were strictly censored–for adults as well as children. Plato's recommended educational techniques do not exactly square with the philosophy expressed by the Supreme Court when it noted that children are not simply "closed circuit recipients of only that which the State chooses to communicate." That a federal appeals court in 1998 relied on Plato's argument for indoctrination in "virtuous thoughts" without apparent irony suggest the extent to which the concept of harm to minors had come to overshadow more libertarian or nuanced judicial approaches to public education.

These two cases aptly illustrated the general lessening of judicial protection for academic freedom in public schools, particularly where the subject matter was "vulgar" or sexual. To list all the major works of literature removed from public schools courses or libraries in the middle and late 1990s would consume many pages; indeed, no work that addressed the human condition was exempt from attack. High on the list would be Maya Angelou's *I Know Why the Caged Bird Sings*, Toni Morrison's *Song of Solomon* and *Beloved*, Gabriel Garcia Marquez's *One Hundred Years of Solitude*, Aldous Huxley's *Brave New World*, Richard Wright's *Native Son*, Arthur Miller's *Death of a Salesman*, J. D. Salinger's *Catcher in the Rye*, and almost anything by Judy Blume. One school board in Oconee County, Georgia, simply finessed the whole process in July 1994 by directing employees to purge school libraries of all books with "explicit sex." That particular episode had a happy ending, though, when protesting citizens, including students carrying signs that said "Reading is fundamental, not fundamentalist," persuaded the board to rescind its order.

The impulse to shield minors from controversial ideas or explicit sexual information has had particularly unfortunate consequences in the field of sex education. Perhaps nowhere else in the public school curriculum is there the same opportunity to give young people health- and life-saving information about safe and responsible sexual behavior. Yet by the mid-1990s sex education in the United States had become such an ideological battlefield that those advocating "abstinence only" curricula were able to pass a federal law that conditioned government aid to local sex education programs on the removal of any references to contraception or abortion. This law further required that students be told that "a mutually faithful monogamous relationship in the context of marriage is the expected standard of human sexual activity," and "sexual activity outside of the context of marriage is likely to have harmful psychological and physical effects."[11]

Although the merits of sexual abstinence for adolescents can probably be debated endlessly, the reality is that a majority of American teenagers are sexually active before their eighteenth birthdays.[12] In light of this reality, medically incomplete and ideologically heavy-handed abstinence-only education will likely cause either snickers of disbelief or feelings of guilt and shame about sexual activity. Ironically, rhetoric about protecting minors in this context has turned into a campaign to harm them in profound physical and psychological ways.

A Word on Child Pornography

One final aspect of the harm-to-minors issue at mid-decade was the politically explosive subject of child pornography. In 1982, the Supreme Court ruled that child pornography is unprotected by the First Amendment, even if it does not meet the three-part obscenity test (see chapter 1), because of society's compelling interest in protecting minors from sexual abuse. This initial rationale for banning child pornography was largely forgotten in the 1990s, as government agencies began to target artistic nude photographs that depicted no sexual activity, and Congress expanded federal law to ban erotic images of young-looking people even if no minor was used in their creation.

Chapter 5 describes the U.S. government's attempt in the early 1990s to prosecute art photographer Jock Sturges for his depictions of children and teenagers, many of them in family groups on nudist beaches in France. Although Sturges's photographs show no sexual activity, prosecutors sought indictments because federal law defines child pornography to include "lewd exhibition of the genitals or pubic area." Sturges's works did not focus on the genitals of his nude subjects but did not coyly obscure them either. A federal grand jury refused to indict.

In the five years that followed, a number of other artists, usually lesser known, became targets of similar criminal or child-protection investigations. In all these cases, the subjects of controversy were nude photographs that were artistic, not pornographic. Yet some government officials evidently thought otherwise. In 1998, pressure groups persuaded prosecutors in Tennessee and Alabama to bring criminal charges against Barnes & Noble bookstores for selling works by Sturges and a British photographer, David Hamilton. Although vowing to defend these cases on First Amendment grounds, by June 1998 Barnes & Noble had brokered a deal with prosecutors in Tennessee and agreed to place the books in question out of the reach of minors.

Political anxiety over pedophilia also led to Congress's passage of the 1996 "Child Pornography Protection Act ("CPPA"), a law that expands the definition of child pornography from depictions of minors engaged in sexual acts to depictions of individuals who *appear to be minors.* The CPPA, moreover, applies not only to photographs of actual young-looking people, but also to drawings or computer-generated images of imaginary young-looking people. The original justification for criminalizing child pornography—the compelling governmental interest in shielding actual minors from abuse—was now replaced by a much more sweeping rationale: that sexualized images of people who appear to be minors must be banned because otherwise they will whet the appetites of pedophiles, with potentially disastrous results. The likelihood that child pornography, like adult pornography, is largely used for cathartic, masturbatory purposes, has not lowered the pitch of this campaign to protect children, at least symbolically, by punishing bad thoughts.

The CPPA amounts to thought control of a type that would immediately be recognized as anathema to free expression if the subject were anything other than child pornography. For on the theory underlying this law, any book, picture, film, or computer communication that describes offensive or harmful behavior could be banned because it might inspire prospective criminals to act. Yet because of the overheated politics of the child pornography issue, the Justice Department was able to persuade a federal court in California to uphold the CPPA. (Another court, in Maine, struck it down.) At this writing, the ultimate judicial fate of the CPPA is still in doubt.

There was a touch of the absurd in another attempted expansion of the concept of child pornography that occurred in 1997. A local advocacy group, Oklahomans for Children and Families, had been trying for months to generate controversy over books or videos available in the Oklahoma City public library. Finally, they happened upon a video of *The Tin Drum*, an Academy Award-winning film version of Günter Grass's celebrated allegorical novel about a boy who is so disgusted with the behavior of adults in Nazi Germany that he refuses to grow up. One fleeting scene in the film suggests an act of oral sex between the boy and his teenage babysitter. Alerted by Oklahomans for Children and Families, the Oklahoma City police sought the advice of a local judge, who viewed the episode and informally declared it to violate the state's child pornography law. (There was no hearing, notice to the other side, or written decision.) The police thereupon seized every copy of the film to be found in Oklahoma City, including tapes rented by video stores whose customer records the police had inspected in likely violation of a federal privacy law.

Three lawsuits resulted from this unusual episode. In a preliminary ruling, a federal judge found the seizures to be unconstitutional. In October 1998, the same judge ruled that the brief erotic extract from *The Tin Drum* did not violate Oklahoma's child pornography law.

Arts Funding

Chapter 6 of *Sex, Sin, and Blasphemy* tackles another highly politicized issue; government arts funding. Since the first major attacks on the National Endowment for the Arts in 1989, complaints about misuse of "the taxpayers' money" have provided fertile ground for cultural battles over provocative artistic work, particularly if it has sexual or religious content. The NEA, on the political defensive throughout the 1990s, saw its budget shrink nearly in half, struggled to avert zero funding, eliminated most grants to individual artists, and became increasingly cautious in those grants it did award.

Meanwhile, two federal courts in a lawsuit brought by Karen Finley and three other performance artists struck down Congress's 1990 mandate that the NEA consider "general standards of decency and respect for the diverse beliefs and values of the American public" in awarding grants. As the U.S. Court of Appeals for the Ninth Circuit explained, this "decency and respect" law was both too vague and too "viewpoint-discriminatory" to be a constitutionally acceptable standard for funding by an agency created not to finance government-approved messages but to support a diversity of artistic expression. Although government of course need not fund art—or any other form of creative or intellectual activity—when it does so, the court of appeals said, it cannot manipulate its funds in a way that favors certain moral or ideological views over others.[13]

The government appealed again, and in March 1998 *NEA v. Finley* was argued by Georgetown University law professor David Cole before the U.S. Supreme Court. I was co-counsel with Cole and sat beside him as he endured a vigorous grilling from the justices. One reason for the judicial skepticism was not difficult to discern, for the NEA by this time was so weakened that every legislative session brought another battle for its existence. Affirming the court of appeals' judgment that the NEA could not disfavor grant applications simply because of their "indecent" or "disrespectful" ideas would undoubtedly provide rhetorical ammunition to those who wished to abolish the agency entirely.

The "decency and respect" law had been a deliberately vague congressional compromise that avoided more specific ideological restrictions—for example, explicit bans on funding any art deemed to promote homosexuality or blasphemy. The law only required the NEA to take "decency and respect" "into consideration." Although Congress's message to the agency was hard to miss, the law was mushy enough to give the justices a way out of their dilemma. Six of them, in an opinion by Sandra Day O'Connor, therefore accepted the Justice Department's argument that the clause was merely advisory, and left the NEA free to operate just as it always had. Should the agency apply the clause "in a manner that raises concern about the suppression of disfavored viewpoints," Justice O'Connor said, it would be time enough to adjudicate a First Amendment challenge.[14]

Justice O'Connor's opinion for the Court in *NEA v. Finley* thus reiterated the longstanding rule that "even in the provision of subsidies, the Government may not aim at the suppression of dangerous ideas."[15] That is, "viewpoint discrimination" in government arts funding is unconstitutional. This was a highly significant point, given both the vociferous disagreement of two justices—Antonin Scalia and Clarence Thomas—who would have imposed no First Amendment restraints at all on arts funding, and the fact that local funding controversies throughout the 1990s were often characterized by explicit viewpoint discrimination. Indeed, in the few months just before the Supreme Court decided *Finley*, two respected cultural organizations, the Esperanza Center in San Antonio, Texas, and Out North Theater in Anchorage, Alaska, lost their funding because of explicit anti-homosexual sentiments voiced by local leaders.

NEA v. Finley was widely reported as a decision permitting the NEA to deny grants based on "indecency," but that was not what the Supreme Court actually said. The Court's majority opinion left open the possibility that rejections on account of perceived indecency—like more obviously viewpoint-based rejections (for example, based on an artist's refusal to endorse the Republican Party platform)—would be unconstitutional. Indeed, all three of the justices who wrote separate opinions in _Finley_ said that "decency" is a viewpoint-based criterion because it turns on questions of "conformity to prevailing standards of propriety."[16] This insight, like the _Finley_ majority's recognition that First Amendment prinicples do apply to government support for art, will be critically important as long as the slogan of "taxpayers' money" continues to be used to attack art that is not tame, safe, or at least 100 years old.

Ultimately, though, judicial rules against viewpoint discrimination cannot protect funding programs from political firestorms unless there is public support for artistic freedom and understanding that art cannot do its job if forced into a "family values" straitjacket. Two unfortunate incidents during the years when _Finley_ was slowly making its way to the Supreme Court dramatized the fundamentally political nature of the issue. In the first incident, in 1993, members of the Cobb County, Georgia Board of Commissioners became incensed over homosexual content in two respected plays—Terrence McNally's _Lips Together, Teeth Apart_, and David Henry Hwang's _M. Butterfly_—that had recently been performed at a local theater that received some county funds. A resolution was proposed endorsing "the traditional family structure" as consonant with community standards, announcing that "the lifestyles advocated by the gay community should not be endorsed by government policymakers," and concluding that "the Board of Commissioners pledges not to fund those activities which seek to contravene these existing community standards." In response to warnings that such viewpoint discrimination would be unconstitutional, the commissioners chose to eliminate arts funding altogether, except for institutions owned by the county.

Four years later in Mecklenburg County, North Carolina, a similar controversy arose over performance of Tony Kushner's Pulitzer Prize-winning play, *Angels in America*, at the Charlotte Repertory Theater. There followed a resolution stating that the Board of County Commissioners was committed to protecting children "from exposure to perverted forms of sexuality," and therefore that the local arts funding agency was being disbanded and all further grants would be awarded by the commissioners themselves. Several months later, the commissioners abandoned arts funding entirely. Although arts fans mounted protests in both of these instances, they were not widely enough supported to persuade the legislators to reinstate funding.

Censorship in the Twenty-first Century

What can we make of these continuing "censorship wars" of the 1990s? Despite astounding developments like the rise of the Internet, and intensified political rhetoric about harm to minors, the unifiying theme of the past five years is remarkably similar to that already identified at a number of points in *Sex, Sin, and Blasphemy*. That is, a sizable portion of the American public accepts censorship as an imagined "quick fix" solution to moral drift and other social ills. This acceptance arises in part, I think, from an intolerance of ambiguity, a disinterest in engaging creative works or pondering the complex ways in which they affect our psyches. Instead of seeing artistic expression as a form of catharsis, an opportunity for vicarious pleasure, or a way of processing insecurity, aggression, and despair, many Americans in 1998, as in 1993, seem to view such expression simply as a cause of bad attitudes and traumatic events. Fears of unbridled violence or sexuality, of a world without clear moral compass, and of the impact that a gigantic multimedia universe is having on our children, have contributed to the continued scapegoating of speech in America.

As columnist Frank Rich commented recently, apropos of a temporarily successful effort by the Catholic League for Religious and Civil Rights to stop a planned production of a new play by Terrence McNally, advocacy groups and politicians across the ideological spectrum have become increasingly thin-skinned about perceived slights to their beliefs and cultural identities. In consequence, Rich said, the practice of attacking, silencing, or defunding art with presumptively offensive ideas has grown ever more popular and accepted. I do not see much hope that this thinning of America's cultural skin is likely to stop anytime soon; the "spin doctor" recommended in the conclusion of *Sex, Sin, and Blasphemy* is still needed. In fact, an army of spin doctors would be more like it.

I am not gloomy or pessimistic, though, because the experience of seven years has taught me that the demand for censorship and the counterbalancing need for understanding about the nature of art, are always in tension. Meanwhile, there is a thriving artistic and intellectual scene in the United States that is fundamentally irrepressible despite the regulations and ratings systems invented to control it. Perhaps more heartening are the young people whose tender psyches have become a political battleground in the 1990s. The ones I have worked with in censorship cases are savvy, original, and keenly appreciative of our unique heritage of First Amendment freedom.

New York City
October 1998

@ INTRODUCTION @

Censorship and Artistic Freedom

*What do we have from the past? Art and thought. That's
what lasts. That's what continues to feed people and give
them an idea of something better.*

—Susan Sontag[1]

I N 1989 STRANGE THINGS BEGAN TO HAPPEN IN THESE United States. Musicians and music store owners were charged with crimes for singing songs or selling tapes and records. The U.S. Congress passed a resolution condemning a major museum for permitting a display that "encourages disrespect for the flag." The federal arts funding agency was accused of blasphemy for assisting an artist whose work dealt with religious themes. A U.S. senator tore to shreds a reproduction of the same artist's work on the Senate floor.

Sex, sin, and blasphemy became major political issues—in the real world but also, increasingly, in the world of art and imagination. Symbols, words, ideas, and images were being blamed for social ills. If only America could rid itself of all those pesky artists, all that crude and irreverent and sometimes violent popular entertainment, surely our social problems would fade away.

And so "censorship" became a key word in political debate. Was it censorship when the National Endowment for the Arts caved in to political pressure and declined to fund artists whose work was controversial? Or was it simply a refusal to sponsor the work—a sensible political choice? Was it censorship to remove books from school libraries because of dirty words, mention of sexual matters, unpatriotic sentiments, or descriptions of the supernatural? Or was it simply an appropriate exercise of discretion by school boards? Was it censorship to charge musicians, filmmakers, museum directors— or nude dancers—with obscenity or other crimes? After all, "obscene" works aren't protected by the First Amendment.

Infusing all these battles over words, images, and symbols was what some observers dubbed an American "culture war"—an explosion of ideological conflict over differing attitudes about sexuality, religion, women's liberation, and "family values." The same cultural and religious opposition to reproductive freedom, for example, or to gay rights, with their implied messages that sexuality may have purposes other than childbearing, also fueled some of the nation's censorship crusades.

Attacks on artists and entertainers have often succeeded because they push "hot buttons"—subjects that arouse emotions so powerful that they may interfere with rational thought. In the recent and ongoing censorship wars, such hot buttons have included sex, especially homosexuality; religion, especially sacred symbols or perceived heresies; race, especially images connecting race with sex or violence; and patriotism, especially if symbols like the American flag are involved.

Along with arguments about censorship have come arguments about artistic freedom and the nature of art. Is there no limit to the liberties of artists and entertainers, even in a free society like ours? Does the First Amendment give absolute protection to freedom of speech? Though the words of the amendment are unequivocal— "Congress shall make *no* law . . . abridging the freedom of speech"— society and the courts have always recognized exceptions: libel and slander, threats, extortion, perjury, fraud, "fighting words," and, at least since the mid-nineteenth century, "obscenity."

This book is a product of the censorship wars. It surveys the different fields of combat, from criminal prosecutions to funding controversies to film ratings and the labeling of music lyrics. It explores both the direct and the subtle ways that censorship happens, that powerful or vocal institutions or pressure groups succeed in silencing or suppressing the ideas, images, and entertainment they find offensive or threatening. And it argues that all Americans need to care about these issues—even if we aren't artists ourselves, even if we personally find some of the art that's attacked objectionable, and even when we're not sure it's "art" at all.

What Is Censorship?

According to Webster's Dictionary, to "censor" means "to examine in order to suppress or delete anything considered objectionable." The word "censor" originated in ancient Rome, where the government appointed officials to take the census and to supervise public morals. Censorship happens whenever some people succeed in imposing their political or moral values on others by suppressing words, images, or ideas that they find offensive.

A censor, traditionally, is an official whose job it is to examine literature, movies, or other forms of creative expression and to remove or ban anything she considers unsuitable. In this definition, censorship is something the government does. But censorship can also be accomplished very effectively by private groups.

Not all forms of censorship are illegal. When private individuals agitate to eliminate TV programs they dislike, or threaten to boycott the companies that support those programs with advertising dollars, they are certainly trying to censor artistic expression and interfere with the free speech of others. But their actions are perfectly legal; in fact, their protests are protected by the First Amendment right to freedom of speech.

Not even all government censorship is unlawful. For example, we still have laws against "obscenity" in art and entertainment. These laws allow the government to punish people for producing or disseminating material about sex, if a judge or jury thinks the material is sufficiently offensive and lacks any "serious value." This "obscenity" exception to the First Amendment is a foolish, archaic, and unfair departure from the principles of free speech. (See Chapter 1 for an explanation of how the obscenity exception to the First Amendment came about, and the problems that arise in trying to figure out what it means.) Until the exception is eliminated, though, our federal and state governments will continue to be able to use their obscenity laws to censor some forms of artistic expression.

What Is Artistic Freedom?

Some readers may be puzzled to see the terms "obscenity" and "artistic expression" in the same sentence. Isn't "obscenity," as defined by our current laws, just a sex aid—pornographic material with no pretense to artistic value? How can obscenity be considered "art"?

Defining "art" (or "good art") and distinguishing it from mere "entertainment" (or "bad art") is a tricky job. As the Supreme Court has recognized, judgments about art are inherently subjective; "one man's vulgarity may be another's lyric."[2] For purposes of free speech, trying to make the distinction is unnecessary, and perhaps even counterproductive. The point about censorship is that neither government nor private pressure groups should be able to mandate standards of content or taste, or to tell Americans what we may see, read, and enjoy in the realm of art *or* entertainment.

Artistic expression, then, for purposes of the censorship debate, should have the broadest possible definition. It should include books, movies, painting, posters, sexy dancing, street theater, graffiti, comics, television, music videos—anything produced by the creative imagination, from Shakespeare to sitcoms, from opera to rock. Freedom of expression may mean that we have to tolerate some art that is offensive, insulting, outrageous, or just plain bad. But it's a small price to pay for the liberty and diversity that form the foundation of a free society.

There was a time when the American legal system didn't recognize artistic expression, especially in its more lowbrow forms, as constitutionally protected speech. Freedom in political debate—the robust and often rude exchange of ideas that's necessary for democratic government—was seen as the only purpose of the First Amendment.

That time is, thankfully, past. Although political debate remains at the top of the "hierarchy" of First Amendment values, the Supreme Court has recognized that "the freedom of speech" also secures our right to artistic expression. As the Court said in 1948 (in a case involving censorship of cheap detective novels), "We reject the suggestion that the constitutional protection for free speech applies only to the exposition of ideas. The line between the informing and the entertaining is too elusive."[3]

Creative works are constitutionally protected in large part because of the critical role they play in a society that values individual autonomy, dignity, and growth. Artistic expression not only provides information and communicates ideas; it also expresses, defines, and nourishes the human personality. Art speaks to our emotions, our intellects, our spiritual lives, and also our physical and sexual lives. Artists celebrate joy and abandon, but they also confront death, depression, and despair. For some of us, rock 'n' roll or rap artists may play these roles and provide these connections; for others, classical composers, sculptors, or playwrights may elicit the most powerful responses.

Of course, artistic expression also contributes to political debate. Art and entertainment often make political statements, document cruel and brutal social conditions, move people to indignation or action. Indeed, it's usually because of controversial political content that art is censored. From the medieval popes who prescribed strict rules for religious paintings to twentieth-century prosecutors who suppressed writings about sex and birth control through obscenity laws, arts censorship has usually had an ideological purpose.

But what if the ideological purpose behind censorship is moral or just? Why should Americans oppose arts censorship when so much of modern entertainment is full of gratuitous violence, when some artwork can be seen as insulting religion, when pornography appears to celebrate promiscuous sex? Why not let the government pass some laws about what can or can't be published, exhibited, read, sold, or displayed? Why not let the political and moral values of the majority of people decide what ideas, themes, performances, and pictures should be allowed?

There are a couple of good reasons why not. First of all, a free society is based on the principle that each individual has a right to decide what art or entertainment she wants to receive—or create. As Supreme Court Justice Sandra Day O'Connor has written, "At the heart of liberty is the right to define one's own concept of existence, of meaning, of the universe, and of the mystery of human life."[4] Neither the majority of people nor a vocal, powerful minority should be able to interfere with this personal autonomy by dictating ideological, religious, or artistic standards.

All censorship contradicts freedom, but there's an additional problem with censorship of the arts: creative expression is inherently ambiguous. This is a point that the censors among us just never seem to get. When televangelists shout their outrage at a movie like *The Last Temptation of Christ*, or at an art photograph like Andres Serrano's *Piss Christ*, because they see these works as blasphemy, they are imposing one-dimensional interpretations on multidimensional creations. The artists who created these works, like many others who explore sacred themes or symbols, are often deeply religious, though their work may not conform to any particular orthodoxy.

Artists often have ambiguous, even contradictory meanings in mind when they write a book or song, paint a picture, or script a TV sitcom. Audiences bring to these musical creations, movies, books, and plays a variety of equally complicated responses. Often works of art and mass entertainment simply reflect the imagination, fears, or fantasies of their creators—or of society. To interpret them literally and reductively is to miss the point. Like the ancient Greeks, who invented tragic theater as a form of catharsis, modern artists and their audiences may respond powerfully to the words, ideas, and images in music, movies, visual art, even pornography, but that doesn't mean they're ready to go out and imitate what they see. Most men who attend a performance of *Oedipus Rex* do not proceed to kill their fathers and marry their mothers.

Creative works sometimes hold a mirror up to society, giving us a chance to reflect on the world, showing us its beauty or confronting us with its injustice and evil. Art isn't always supposed to be comfortable or comforting; yet because it may reflect cruel realities doesn't mean that it advocates cruelty. And suppressing those words and images won't make the realities go away.

Copycat Lawsuits

A series of lawsuits that began in the 1970s has dramatized the problem that lies at the heart of the censorship debate: the tendency to blame artistic expression for real-world pain. On one side of the conflict are those who literally believe that unstable individuals "copy" the acts or ideas they see in works of art or journalism, and that the way to prevent such copying is to punish and censor the artists, producers, and journalists involved. On the other side are those who would hold the criminals responsible for their acts, and leave art free to document, to protest, to advocate, to inform, and to explore.

One of the early copycat lawsuits was brought by the parents of a young man against three television networks. The parents claimed that their son had been desensitized to violence by watching too much TV, and, as a result, had cold-bloodedly murdered an eighty-three-year-old woman.

A federal court dismissed the suit, saying that allowing the claim to go forward would violate the First Amendment. If this kind of case could be brought, the judge wrote, then broadcasters would be "in jeopardy for televising Hamlet, Julius Caesar, Grimm's Fairy Tales; more contemporary offerings such as All Quiet on the Western Front, and even The Holocaust, and indeed would render John Wayne a risk not acceptable to any but the boldest broadcasters."[5] This judge applied the Supreme Court's "direct incitement" legal standard, as set forth in a 1969 decision called *Brandenburg* v. *Ohio*. Under that rule, even incendiary speech, even speech that advocates crime, can only be punished when it reaches the level of direct incitement to imminent lawless action. Here, said the judge, there was no evidence that the young man was "'incited' or goaded into unlawful behavior by a particular call to action."

The "direct incitement" standard is an important shield against censorship. Like Justice Oliver Wendell Holmes's famous example of "falsely shouting fire in a theater and causing a panic," incitement must have an element of immediacy and emergency about it. When there's time to think, when there's time for the many elements of individual character and motivation to intervene, then an article, film, picture, or speech, even one that advocates violence, can't be punished or suppressed. If the law were otherwise, art and literature from the Bible to Shakespeare could be condemned on the theory that it inspired some unstable person to commit an unlawful act.

Nevertheless, lawyers representing bereaved families continue to try to hold authors and publishers responsible for so-called copy-cat crimes. In the late 1970s, NBC was sued for broadcasting a film called *Born Innocent*, about the traumas suffered by an adolescent girl who had become a ward of the state. In one scene the girl is violently attacked and raped with a "plumber's helper." The parents of a child who was later raped with a bottle sued NBC, claiming the TV film inspired the attack on their daughter. Again, the court recognized the grim implications for free speech if this kind of claim were allowed to proceed. The threat of damages liability—even the anticipated cost of defending a lawsuit that you may ultimately win—can be a powerful tool of censorship. The court quoted Justice Louis Brandeis: "Among free men, the deterrents ordinarily to be applied to prevent crime are education and punishment for violations of the law, not abridgement of the rights of free speech."[6]

In 1981 *Penthouse* magazine was sued by the mother of a fourteen-year-old boy who died tragically, apparently while engaging in "autoerotic asphyxiation." *Penthouse* had published an article on the subject, replete with warnings about the dangers of imitating the activities described. The plaintiff claimed that the warnings were mere window dressing, and that the article had incited her son to kill himself accidentally while trying to attain the orgasmic heights suggested by the magazine. The mother won before a sympathetic jury.

A federal appeals court reversed the jury verdict. Analyzing the First Amendment issue in light of the Supreme Court standard, the judges ruled that the *Penthouse* article was protected by the First Amendment because it didn't come anywhere close to being a direct incitement to imminent harmful action.

Another case was brought in the late eighties against the manufacturers of Dungeons and Dragons by parents of a boy who, they claimed, had become so obsessed by the game that he could no longer separate fantasy from reality and was "driven to self-destruction." Although many parents are understandably frustrated by the endless hours their kids spend on "D&D," and may sympathize with the plaintiffs in this case, the court rightly dismissed the suit on First Amendment grounds.

Rock musicians have been particular targets of copycat lawsuits. In 1990 the British heavy metal band Judas Priest stood trial for seventeen days in Nevada, charged with responsibility for a suicide pact. One of the two boys involved, who survived, testified that he and his friend had listened repeatedly to the group's song "Dream Deceiver." There was extensive evidence that the boys' families were dysfunctional, that their problems were caused by violence and substance abuse within their homes, and by psychological factors long predating the boys' intoxication with Judas Priest. But, as one music critic observed, for these families, rock music made "an easy scapegoat." A "sensationalized rock lyric, however goofy and harmless, can overshadow very real and serious problems."[7]

Two years earlier, grieving parents had unsuccessfully sued Ozzy Osbourne and CBS Records, claiming that Osbourne's song "Suicide Solution" on the album *Blizzard of Oz* contained direct as well as subliminal messages that caused their young son to commit suicide. The court found no subliminal messages and said that the First Amendment "shields all who write, perform, or disseminate . . . music," even if their creations are "aberrant, unpopular and even revolutionary." Any other rule of law would "open a Pandora's box and chill the flow of protected speech."[8]

How Does Arts Censorship Happen? (A Roadmap)

Censorship of artistic expression happens most directly and obviously when the government uses the heavy artillery of criminal law to punish speech. Usually, the criminal charges are based on "obscenity" or "harmful to minors" laws. ("Harmful to minors" laws are sometimes known as "obscene as to minors" laws because they ban the sale of a broader range of sexual material to minors than do adult obscenity laws.)

Obscenity laws are used to attack everything from plain pornography that has few artistic aspirations and frankly serves the purpose of sexual arousal, to serious creations like the musical comedy *Oh! Calcutta!*, works by the late art photographer Robert Mapplethorpe, or rap music by 2 Live Crew and other groups. **Chapter 1** gives a short history and guide to the obscenity exception to the First Amendment, and points up a few of its more glaring defects.

Another form of censorship comes in the guise of government licensing, preclearance, or mandatory labeling. In the thirties, forties, and fifties, many city and state governments had movie censorship boards with the power to review films in advance of exhibition and to ban those considered undesirable. Today, as a result of Supreme Court decisions, most of those boards have disbanded. But nongovernmental classification schemes, like the Motion Picture Association of America's rating system, censor artists indirectly by forcing them to cut dialogue or whole scenes from their films. **Chapter 2,** "Censoring the Dream Factory," describes America's unusual legacy of movie censorship.

The government can also censor without imposing licensing requirements or actually bringing criminal charges. Prosecutors or police departments often need only suggest to local music, book, or video store owners that some of their wares might violate the state obscenity law—most businesses will readily take the hint. Through this method of subtle or not-so-subtle threats, the government can effectively ban works that have never been declared obscene or otherwise unlawful. **Chapter 3** describes how this type of "censorship by suggestion" works.

By 1990, censorship of art through the indirect means of classification and labeling had made its mark on the music business. The recording industry's voluntary "Parental Advisory/Explicit Lyrics" labels have a censoring effect because prosecutors and pressure groups rely on these labels to single out certain types of music for criminal charges or threats. Yet the labels have no legal standing as indications of what can or can't be sold to minors or anybody else. By attaching warning labels to music, companies are inviting censorship.

Rap and rock music express the culture of young people and ethnic minorities. The styles and messages of these pop music forms are not always to the liking of more established groups in society. The attack on rap music in particular, with its sometimes angry messages of black pride and political rebellion, epitomizes the cultural rifts at the heart of so many of our current censorship battles. **Chapter 4** talks about the oddity of trying to censor popular music through labeling or any other scheme.

Laws against "public indecency" or "public nudity" are another way that art gets censored. In the wake of the Supreme Court's 1991 decision allowing states to ban nude dancing, nudity has emerged as a serious competitor to "obscenity" for censorship efforts. Yet the nude human form, in all its variety, versatility, and expressiveness, has always been a major subject of art.

Even without relying on public nudity laws, many government and privately owned theater and exhibition spaces around the country have taken to prohibiting nudity—especially frontal male nudity—in painting, sculpture, and photography. **Chapter 5,** "Getting Naked," talks about why the human body remains such a perennial hot-button issue.

Another type of censorship comes when strings are attached to government funding or benefit programs. Probably the best-known example involves the National Endowment for the Arts. Since 1989 the NEA has been the target of continuing ideological attacks because it funded artists or helped mount exhibits or shows that some groups thought were "pornographic" or insulting to religion. All too frequently, the NEA responded to these attacks not by defending the merit of the art in question but by trying to dissociate itself from projects that might cause controversy.

This is probably not a great way to run an arts agency. Agreeing to ideological, religious, or moral litmus tests for arts grants is dangerous because Americans have a multitude of different views about what is pornographic, blasphemous, or otherwise offensive, indecent, or unpatriotic. Artistic merit can't really be determined by majority vote. And since the government not only funds art but supports libraries, universities, health programs, scientific research, and public parks, allowing public officials to exclude or dictate particular viewpoints just because the government pays the bill would radically restrict the American people's access to ideas and information.

All of these matters are explored in **Chapter 6,** "The Taxpayers' Money."

Still another form of censorship results from pressure campaigns against those TV shows, films, books, or music that a particular political or religious group dislikes. Often, these groups invoke that hot-button word, "pornography." Today in many communities, relatively small groups can exert powerful pressure on government officials to close down or severely limit access to sexual art or entertainment.

Yet pornography is part of a long tradition in art and literature. Since so much creative expression dealing with the all-important subject of sex is attacked and dismissed these days under the accusatory heading of pornography, it's important to demystify the term—to understand what porn is, in all its infinite variety, what purposes it serves, and whether any of the claims made against it should be credited. **Chapter 7**, "The Dreaded 'P' Word," confronts the pornography issue.

"Blasphemy, Subversiveness, and Other Sins," the subject of **Chapter 8**, is a reminder that not *all* current censorship battles concern sex and nudity. The "taxpayers" controversy, after all, began with a religious image, not a sexual one (Andres Serrano's beautiful and much-misunderstood photograph, *Piss Christ*). Intense emotional battles have been fought over the use of American flag symbols in art. School boards are regularly pressured to ban books dealing with "secular humanist" values or "the occult"—that is, aspects of the supernatural that some Christian denominations find subversive or threatening. And "law and order" groups have reacted ferociously to some of the subversive political messages of rock and rap music.

The continuing attacks on religious or political messages that deviate from some presumed American norm demonstrate that much more is at stake in the censorship wars than freedom to talk and think about sex.

❧ I ❧

"Obscenity":
The First Amendment's Second-class Citizen

Sex has occupied a central role in human artistic creations from the very beginning of recorded history. Sexual symbolism, notably the phallus, played an important part in primitive magic and religious rituals, especially fertility rites.

— M. Carmilly-Weinberger[1]

N 1968 A FIRST AMENDMENT LAWYER NAMED CHARLES Rembar wrote a book optimistically titled *The End of Obscenity*. In it, he described his adventures in the world of constitutional law, defending such twentieth-century literary classics as *Tropic of Cancer* and *Lady Chatterley's Lover*. He predicted that because of recent Supreme Court decisions liberalizing the law of obscenity, the long, dark era of prosecuting people for writing or publishing erotic literature would soon be over.

Mr. Rembar proved to be overly optimistic. In 1973, by a slim 5–4 majority, the U.S. Supreme Court, in a case called *Miller* v. *California*, rejected arguments for ending the dubious enterprise of banning, suppressing, and throwing people in jail for disseminating material with sexual themes. Sex—a subject of great importance and near-universal fascination—remained a second-class citizen, receiving separate, and very unequal, treatment under the First Amendment.

Today, sex is the hottest of hot-button issues, the most frequent target of arts censorship crusades. Sometimes, we even face censorship battles over depictions of simple human nudity, which is probably the most significant subject for painting and sculpture in Western art. And the court decisions denying First Amendment protection to a vaguely defined category of speech about sex—so-called obscenity—have provided legal and rhetorical fuel for these crusades.

How have we come to this state of affairs? Speech about sex was not always a second-class citizen. Although governments throughout history have tried to control creative expression, until the nineteenth century the focus was on blasphemy (criticizing the church) and sedition (criticizing the state), rather than eroticism. And the First Amendment protects free expression in sweeping terms. To establish an exception to the First Amendment's guarantee of artistic and intellectual freedom, the government usually has to come up with some "compelling state interest"—for example, a "clear and present danger" that the speech will incite imminent violence. But when it comes to obscenity, our Supreme Court has said that a vague, speculative interest in morality is sufficient to legalize censorship.

What Is "Obscenity," Anyway?

As always, it helps at the outset to figure out what we are talking about. Terms like "obscenity" and "pornography" are thrown around these days quite loosely, whether the discussion is about television, school library books, movies, government funding for the arts, or exhibits at the local museum. These terms are not interchangeable, and their meanings are fluid and subjective.

"Obscenity" has both a common and a legal meaning. ("Pornography," by contrast, is not a legal term. See Chapter 7, "The

Dreaded 'P' Word," for more on its meaning.) Some citizens may think war is obscene; others may think the Iran-Contra affair or the government's bailout of the savings and loan industry were obscene. But in legal parlance, obscenity is a category of speech—speech about sex—that falls outside the protection of the First Amendment. Or so, at least, the Supreme Court has said; many legal scholars find no basis in history or logic for this "obscenity exception" to the First Amendment.

Ever since the Supreme Court began to deal with this issue in the late 1950s, it has struggled for a definition of obscenity. In a 1942 case called *Chaplinsky* v. *New Hampshire*, involving not sex but a heated exchange of insults on a city street, the Court said that some categories of speech are simply "no essential part of any exposition of ideas, and are of such slight social value as a step to truth that any benefit that may be derived from them is clearly outweighed by the social interest in order and morality." In addition to "fighting words" (the insults involved in *Chaplinsky*), the Court named three other types of speech as lacking First Amendment protection because they also, presumably, had "slight social value as a step to truth": libel, profanity, and "the lewd and obscene."

The idea that certain types of speech don't merit First Amendment protection because of their "slight social value as a step to truth" has crumbled in the years since the *Chaplinsky* decision. For example, the celebrated 1964 Supreme Court case of *New York Times Co.* v. *Sullivan* established that First Amendment principles limit the availability and scope of lawsuits for libel.

Sullivan was the segregationist police chief of Montgomery, Alabama; he sued the *New York Times* and won massive damages because of minor factual errors in an ad that the *Times* ran supporting civil rights marchers. The Supreme Court reversed the libel judgment, saying that the First Amendment protected "uninhibited, robust, and wide-open" criticism of public officials—at least unless it could be shown that the critic was deliberately lying or showed "reckless disregard" for the truth. So much for *Chaplinsky's* flat "libel" exception to the First Amendment.

Seven years later, the "profanity" exception was eliminated. This was in *Cohen* v. *California*, otherwise known as the "fuck the draft" case. A Vietnam War protester had been arrested, and criminally convicted, for wearing a jacket that had this no-nonsense slogan emblazoned on it. The Supreme Court, overturning the conviction, ruled that the profane message was protected by the First Amendment. The Court pointed out that a speaker's choice of particular words in expressing a political point can be as important as the point itself, that words have "emotive" as well as "cognitive" value.

Cohen established that the Constitution protected profane words. So much for *that* exception to the First Amendment.

As for the "lewd and obscene," there was little historical basis for the Supreme Court's assertion in *Chaplinsky* that the First Amendment wasn't intended to protect this type of speech. As Supreme Court Justice William O. Douglas observed, the Bill of Rights was "the product of a robust, not a prudish age": none of the founders of the United States, said Douglas, was concerned "with the question of pornography." *Memoirs of a Woman of Pleasure* (otherwise known as *Fanny Hill*) was only the most famous and popular of a number of eighteenth-century pornographic literary classics, among them Benjamin Franklin's *Advice to a Young Man Choosing a Mistress*. Douglas said that Thomas Jefferson and James Madison "would be appalled" at the idea of an "obscenity" exception to the First Amendment.[2]

In England and the United States, there weren't any specific laws against obscenity until the nineteenth century. Before that, only a few isolated criminal prosecutions were even attempted, based on general notions of "immorality." One such prosecution in 1708, for "obscene libel," was dismissed when the court decided there was no such crime. Since the work in question, *Fifteen Plagues of a Maidenhead,* did not insult the Church, the government, or any individual, the court ruled that no harm had been done.

Despite this absence of any historical basis for an obscenity exception to the First Amendment, laws banning "obscene," "indecent," "lewd," or "lascivious" books and pictures came into vogue in the nineteenth century, spurred by private organizations in both England and America that were dedicated to stamping out "vice." These Victorian-era morality campaigns promoted a single ideological view of female sexuality, namely that it hardly existed—or certainly shouldn't in "nice" girls.

The driving force behind the American moral crusade was one Anthony Comstock, founder of the New York Society for the Suppression of Vice, whose slogans were "Morals, not Art and Literature!" and "Books are feeders for brothels!"[3] Comstock campaigned tirelessly for censorship laws not only to stamp out erotic subject matter in art or literature but to suppress information about sexuality, reproduction, and birth control. In 1873 he persuaded Congress (after less than one hour of debate) to pass a law that banned the mailing of materials found to be "lewd," "indecent," "filthy," or "obscene." This Comstock Law remains on the books today, although the ban on information about birth control has been eliminated.

When obscenity laws were used in the nineteenth century, American courts simply assumed that they were valid. This included the Supreme Court, which ruled in 1896 that the federal Comstock Law didn't cover vulgar insults. The Court offered no comment on whether the law violated the Constitution's free speech guarantee—probably because such an idea did not even occur to the justices. First Amendment jurisprudence is a distinctly twentieth-century phenomenon.

Obscenity cases in those early days, and well into the twentieth century, were governed by an 1868 English ruling called *Regina* v. *Hicklin*. The legal definition for obscenity devised in *Hicklin* was "whether the tendency of the matter charged as obscenity is to deprave and corrupt those whose minds are open to such immoral influences and into whose hands a publication of this sort may fall." Thus, under *Hicklin*, if the government thought that children, young women, mentally handicapped individuals, or even potential sociopaths might be "depraved and corrupted" by erotic material, the work could be suppressed, regardless of its value, and the artist could be prosecuted and jailed.

As Justice Felix Frankfurter once commented, the *Hicklin* obscenity standard reduced the adult reading public to what was considered fit for children. Surely, quipped Frankfurter, "this is to burn the house to roast the pig."[4]

Finally, in 1957, the question whether the First Amendment permitted obscenity prosecutions was squarely presented to the U.S. Supreme Court. In that case, *Roth* v. *United States*, a majority of the justices ruled that an obscenity exception to the First Amendment does exist—and relied on the same reasoning it had used in the *Chaplinsky* case fifteen years before. That is, "obscenity" has no value "as a step to truth." In the words of the *Roth* decision, "obscenity" is speech about sex that is "utterly without redeeming social importance."[5] But Justice William Brennan, writing in *Roth*, emphasized that not all art and literature about sex lacks constitutional protection: sex, said Brennan, is "a great and mysterious motive force in human life," and "has indisputably been a subject of absorbing interest to mankind through the ages."[6]

The problem, of course, is where to draw the line. Who decides what informational or creative material is "utterly without redeeming social importance"? And how? How is anybody to locate the elusive boundary that separates obscenity from constitutionally protected art and other speech about sex? After all, in 1957 when *Roth* was decided, it was still a violation of the federal obscenity law to distribute contraceptives or information about their use. The Supreme Court itself, in a bit of inspired understatement, acknowledged six years after *Roth* that the line separating obscenity from constitutionally protected speech is "dim and uncertain."

By the early 1960s, the Supreme Court had settled on three markers to help locate that dim and uncertain barrier. To fit within the obscenity exception to the First Amendment, the Court said (in a case liberating *Fanny Hill* from censorship), a work must be "patently offensive"; it must, taken as a whole, appeal to the "prurient interest"; and its contents must be "utterly without redeeming social value." Apparently, the Court was trying to devise a definition that separated "good" literature or art from "bad" pornography—material without much pretension to artistic value, and merely designed for sexual arousal.

The "utterly without redeeming social value" standard inspired what one observer has called a "post-*Roth* glasnost in obscenity law. For if obscenity was utterly devoid of social value, it was an immediate corollary that anything that was *not* utterly devoid of social value, no matter how salacious, was ipso facto not obscene."[7] First Amendment lawyers quickly took advantage of the Court's new tolerance for art about sex, and secured a steady stream of reversals of obscenity convictions.

Roth and its aftermath inspired lawyers like Charles Rembar to predict the coming "end of obscenity" as a legal issue. But then in 1973 came *Miller* v. *California,* and instead of doing away with obscenity laws, the Supreme Court made criminal convictions *easier* to obtain by loosening the three-part obscenity test.

The Test for "Obscenity" Today

The *Miller* decision made obscenity prosecutions easier in two ways. First, instead of proving that a work of art or literature was "utterly without redeeming social value," prosecutors now had only to prove that the material "lacked serious literary, artistic, political or scientific value." This is known in legal shorthand as the "SLAPS" test.

How judges and juries are supposed to make this judgment is anybody's guess. Certainly, in announcing an "obscenity" definition that allowed the government, through its prosecutors, judges, and juries, to pass judgment on the value of artistic works, the Supreme Court in *Miller* ignored its own earlier warning that "it is largely because government officials cannot make principled distinctions in this area that the Constitution leaves matters of taste and style so largely to the individual."[8]

The second way that the Supreme Court in *Miller* v. *California* made obscenity prosecutions easier had to do with the other two parts of the legal definition: proof that the material was patently offensive and that, taken as a whole, it appealed to a prurient interest in sex. Under pre-*Miller* law, judges and juries had to apply a national standard in applying these two prongs of the obscenity test. But in the new world created by *Miller*, the definition of obscenity could change with locale. Judges and juries could now rely on statewide or even local community mores in deciding whether a book or movie depicted sex in a patently offensive way, or whether, taken as a whole, it appealed to the "prurient interest." So a work could be obscene, illegal, and enough to send people to jail in one town, but entitled to full constitutional protection in the next. Then-Chief Justice Burger, who wrote the majority opinion in *Miller*, explained this anomaly by saying that he didn't see any reason why "the people of Maine or Mississippi" had to "accept public depiction of conduct found tolerable in Las Vegas or New York City."[9]

When he made this statement, Justice Burger evidently forgot that the First Amendment protects us all against the occasional oppressiveness of majority rule, that is, the unfortunate tendency of so many human beings to try to impose their values—in this case, their particular moral and aesthetic values—on others. Under our Constitution, one lone bibliophile or film fanatic in Maine or Mississippi ought to have the same right to receive the information, ideas, and entertainment she chooses as those sinful folks in Las Vegas and New York.

One of the excruciating ironies of the *Miller* case is that in the years just preceding, the Supreme Court really did seem poised to do away with obscenity laws. But the resignation of Justice Arthur Goldberg in 1965, at the behest of President Lyndon Johnson, to become U.S. ambassador to the United Nations, and the subsequent resignation of his successor, Abe Fortas, in 1969, partly because of attacks on his anti-censorship votes in obscenity cases, allowed President Richard Nixon to appoint Warren Burger in 1969 as Chief Justice. Burger provided the one vote needed to *expand* obscenity laws rather than to eliminate them.

What Is "Harmful to Minors"?

Miller v. *California* established a three-part test purporting to define what art and entertainment is so patently offensive or lacking in serious value that states (or the federal government) can bar adults from reading or viewing it. The test is vague—hopelessly so—but it does narrow the scope of material that can be censored. It recognizes that sex is an important subject and the First Amendment gives us the right to think, write, read, talk, and even sing about it. Most of what's drawn, filmed, or written about sex can't be banned.

But what about children? Can the government set up different standards to prevent sexually explicit material from getting into the hands of those who may be too young to understand it? Five years before *Miller*, the Supreme Court said yes, and upheld a New York State law that made it a crime to disseminate to anyone under eighteen material that was described as "harmful to minors."

The question, of course, is what such a vague term as "harmful to minors" means. The Court said works that were "harmful to minors" (or "obscene as to minors") had to be about sex and had to meet a modified version of the adult obscenity test. What this means today is that for a successful criminal prosecution under a "harmful to minors" law, material has to appeal to the "prurient interest" of minors, lack serious value for minors, and be "patently offensive," according to prevailing standards among adults regarding what's fit for minors.

The problem of figuring out what all this means is even worse for "harmful to minors" than for adult obscenity laws, because a minor is generally anybody under eighteen. Seventeen-year-olds are obviously capable of enjoying, comprehending, and making rational judgments about a great deal of art and entertainment that might be boring, befuddling, scary, or threatening to ten-year-olds, and of no interest at all to four-year-olds. Some youths of seventeen are even in college, studying such esoteric subjects as semiotics and deconstruction. Surely *Debbie Does Dallas* won't hurt them. And as the Supreme Court has recognized, teenagers—even children—do have First Amendment rights.

As a result of all this, the problems of vagueness, and arbitrary enforcement, that plague all obscenity laws, are multiplied when it comes to laws governing what's harmful to minors. Recent prosecutions and legislative proposals for restricting minors' access to "explicit lyrics" in popular music have dramatized these problems. (See Chapter 4, "The Devil's Music," for details.)

A Word about "Indecency"

Just to make matters even more complicated, the courts have recognized yet another category of speech about sex that, although not obscene, can nevertheless sometimes be regulated: "indecency."

Indecency law got its start in 1978 with a Supreme Court decision called *Federal Communications Commission v. Pacifica.* Pacifica radio in New York City had broadcast a satiric "Filthy Words" monologue in which the comedian George Carlin repeated, discussed, intoned, analyzed, and joked about seven words that the FCC had banned from the airwaves. The original list, for reasons perhaps known only to the FCC, were: shit, piss, fuck, cunt, cocksucker, motherfucker, and tits. Carlin pointed out, among other things, that the list was redundant because the word "fuck" was already contained in the compound term "motherfucker."

Carlin's plain purpose was to demystify the words by repeating them. His routine was an attempt to examine and satirize the mores of a society (and a government) that tries to censor the use of common terms for body parts and functions while permitting fancy circumlocutions. The FCC, following its legal mandate to prevent any "obscene, indecent, or profane language by means of radio communications," imposed sanctions on the radio station. Pacifica protested to the courts that the words, and the monologue, were constitutionally protected.

In a narrow and tortured decision, the Supreme Court said it was okay for the FCC to punish Pacifica for broadcasting the seven dirty words during a time when children were likely to be in the

listening audience. Certainly a monologue like Carlin's was constitutionally protected speech; it did not meet the standard for legal
obscenity. But because of the limited number of frequencies that
were available, the FCC already had much more power to regulate
broadcasting than any arm of government would ordinarily have
over other forms of communication. And in the interests of protecting children from the supposed harms that would befall them
were they to hear these venerable Anglo-Saxon terms, the commission could require radio and television stations to "channel" so-
called indecent speech into the late-night hours.

In disciplining Pacifica, the FCC relied on a definition of indecency as "language that describes, in terms patently offensive as
measured by contemporary community standards for the broadcast
medium, sexual or excretory activities or organs." With only minor
changes, this is still the government's indecency standard: its definition of material that broadcasters must channel to a "safe harbor"
nighttime period when it is least likely that children will be listening. And because the standard has been accepted for purposes of
FCC regulation of broadcasting, would-be censors have used it in
other laws or proposals: to regulate, for example, "dial-a-porn" tele-
phone services, federal arts funding, and cable television. "Patently
offensive depictions or descriptions of sexual or excretory activities
or organs" has become standard rhetoric in the censorship wars.

Unfortunately, however, nobody really knows what it means.
Like the three-part obscenity standard, this one-part definition of
indecency is hopelessly subjective and vague. What is patently
offensive to a fundamentalist minister may seem tame stuff indeed
to an avant-garde arts audience. What passes for indecency in a
conservative rural community may be wholly unexceptional in a
cosmopolitan city. What an upper-class white heterosexual family
views as objectionable, whether on the broadcast spectrum, on

cable, or in the arts, may be the normal style of discourse for poor or minority inner-city youths.

Because "patently offensive" is such an elastic and, ultimately, meaningless term in a heterogeneous society like ours, indecency laws have the effect of inhibiting *any* expression about "sexual or excretory activities or organs," from broadcasts of readings by Allen Ginsberg, one of the true titans of twentieth-century American poetry, to the "shock jock" morning radio broadcasts of Howard Stern, whose impertinent bathroom humor led to punitive FCC fines in late 1992. Indecency laws have thus become a dubious, highly malleable new source of censorship power for those frustrated by the limits of obscenity law under *Miller* v. *California*.

A Historical Digression

Though "obscenity" today may conjure up an image of sleazy porn flicks without pretense to artistic value, the history of obscenity prosecutions suggests how they have consistently been used to suppress genuine creative works. Books banned from the U.S. mails under the Comstock Law included many of the greatest classics written over the several thousand years of human civilization: Aristophanes's *Lysistrata*, Rabelais's *Gargantua*, Chaucer's *Canterbury Tales*, Boccaccio's *Decameron*, and even *The Arabian Nights*. The list of modern authors whose books have been banned under federal and state obscenity laws reads like a literary honor role: Honoré de Balzac, Victor Hugo, Oscar Wilde, Ernest Hemingway, John Dos Passos, Eugene O'Neill, James Joyce, D. H. Lawrence, Clifford Odets, Erskine Caldwell, John Steinbeck, William Faulkner, F. Scott Fitzgerald, Theodore Dreiser, Richard Wright, Norman Mailer, Edmund Wilson, Sinclair Lewis, Ralph Ellison, and Walt Whitman—to name just a few. Anthony Comstock boasted in 1874 that the previous year's Comstock Law had enabled him to destroy more than 194,000 pictures, 134,000 pounds of books, 5,500 sets of playing cards, and 60,300 "rubber articles."[10] In the early 1900s, theater works from George Bernard Shaw's *Mrs. Warren's Profession* to the Yiddish playwright Sholem Asch's *God of Vengeance* were censored or banned, and the actors arrested, because the works dealt with such forbidden subjects as prostitution or homosexuality.

Obscenity laws haven't merely been used to attack great art and literature. Those who enforced the federal Comstock Law and its state equivalents also had a political agenda: to impose Victorian codes on social behavior, especially the behavior of women, by suppressing information about birth control, reproductive freedom, and sexuality. Before the 1870s, contraceptives, though rarely very effective, had at least been widely available. Once obscenity laws were enacted, Comstock and others used them both to confiscate the devices themselves and to suppress information or advocacy on the subject.

Margaret Sanger, America's most tireless champion of birth control, was dogged by Comstock, his successor, John Sumner, and other "decency" police, throughout her career. In 1913, Comstock prosecuted Sanger for her writings on sexuality and birth control. She was criminally prosecuted again in 1916 and jailed for operating a birth control clinic in Brooklyn. In 1929 she was prohibited from speaking in Boston. She had to sneak diaphragms into the country, as the U.S. Customs Service prohibited their importation.[11] Sanger's career is an object lesson in the ideological use of obscenity laws to suppress women's liberation and sexual freedom.

Sex educator Mary Ware Dennett was also prosecuted and convicted, in 1930, for her book, *The Sex Side of Life*. This was a tame, moralistic manual of elementary anatomy and marital love. A federal appeals court reversed the conviction, noting that anything written about sex "is capable in some circumstances of arousing lust," but that this was hardly justification for banning "any instruction of the young in sex matters," since the alternative was for them to "grope about in mystery and morbid curiosity," and acquire their sex education "from ill-informed and often foul-mouthed companions."[12]

The ideological bias of obscenity prosecutions was also evident in both English and American cases involving *The Well of Loneliness*, a mawkish yet powerfully moving novel about a lesbian's struggle for acceptance and self-respect. The book was found obscene even though it had no explicit descriptions of sex. Expert testimony on its literary worth, offered in the English trial by Virginia Woolf and other major writers of the day, was rejected by the court as irrelevant. A New York court in 1929 ruled *The Well of Loneliness* obscene—even though the judge acknowledged that the book was "a well written, carefully constructed piece of fiction" with "no unclean words"—simply because it drew a sympathetic portrait of homosexuality, and "pleads for tolerance on the part of society."[13]

Even adultery was not a subject tolerated by obscenity enforcers. In 1959 the Supreme Court overturned a ban on a film inspired by D. H. Lawrence's novel *Lady Chatterley's Lover* because the New York censorship board had disapproved of the movie's message. Justice Potter Stewart wrote:

> The First Amendment's basic guarantee is of the freedom to advocate ideas. . . . Its guarantee is not confined to the expression of ideas that are conventional or shared by a majority. It protects advocacy of the opinion that adultery may sometimes be proper, no less than advocacy of socialism or the single tax.[14]

It wasn't until the mid 1930s that the legal reign of Comstockery began to ebb, with two decisions: in one the court overturned Mary Ware Dennett's conviction for *The Sex Side of Life*, and in the other, the celebrated *Ulysses* case, the American Civil

Liberties Union persuaded a federal judge that James Joyce's ground-breaking novel was "more emetic than aphrodisiac," and therefore not obscene under the prevailing legal standard.

Yet even after *Ulysses*, obscenity law marched on. The 1957 *Roth* decision, which established the "obscenity exception" to the First Amendment, involved British artist Aubrey Beardsley's illustrations to the myth of Venus and Tannhäuser—a timeless story of an artist's struggle between sensuality and spirituality, which had inspired Richard Wagner to compose one of his steamier operas a century before.

Even after *Roth*, the State of Ohio used obscenity law to ban a highbrow French film, *The Lovers*, by the art film director Louis Malle. The movie told of a bored, neglected bourgeois wife who falls for an irreverent young student. Although it lyrically celebrates the glories of adulterous love, *The Lovers'* sexual explicitness is limited to a fleeting glimpse of the heroine's breast. In 1968 the Supreme Court reversed the obscenity conviction of the Ohio theater owner who exhibited *The Lovers*.

Not only arty European films were at risk. The mainstream American feature *Carnal Knowledge*, starring Candice Bergen, Jack Nicholson, Ann-Margret, and Art Garfunkel, was not just prosecuted but convicted of obscenity (in Georgia) in 1972. On appeal two years later, the Supreme Court reversed the conviction, relying on favorable reviews of the film and the justices' own personal viewing. Justice Rehnquist wrote that nothing in *Carnal Knowledge* met the "patently offensive" standard—despite the Court's statement the year before in *Miller* that such judgments were to be made by local juries.

What's Wrong with the Obscenity Exception to the First Amendment?

The slim majority of five justices who decided *Miller* in 1973 evidently hoped that their new emphasis on community standards would free them of the undignified, often mind-numbing task of reviewing an endless stream of erotic books and movies to determine if they passed all three parts of the obscenity test. That's because two parts of the test would now be left to local choice.

The *Carnal Knowledge* case the very next year suggested that *Miller* wouldn't have the benign result the justices hoped for. And so it turned out: the reliance on community standards has encouraged local crusades against sexually oriented films or literature that would clearly be tolerated in most parts of the nation. And the broadening of the obscenity standard, especially the third part of the test ("serious literary, artistic, political or scientific value") has inspired prosecutors to go after a wider range of material than they might have considered in pre-*Miller* days, in the hope that a jury will be sufficiently offended to decide that the work lacks "serious value."

So obscenity law marches on. Prosecutors in recent years have used both state and federal obscenity bans to crack down on adult book and video stores, distributors, and even producers. Cases have been brought or threatened against live theater companies, and rap and rock music have become targets. Often, a district attorney or police chief has only to threaten prosecution, or notify local music, book, or video stores that certain merchandise is considered obscene or harmful to minors, and the offending material will quietly disappear. (See Chapter 3, "Censorship by Suggestion," for more on how this occurs.)

And when the temperature rises—as it did in 1989 when the National Endowment for the Arts first came under fire—even museum directors aren't safe. (See Chapter 6, "The Taxpayers' Money," for description of the arts funding controversy.) In 1990, at the height of a full-scale assault on the federal arts funding agency, Ohio prosecutors saw fit to charge a Cincinnati museum director,

Dennis Barrie, with the crime of "pandering obscenity" because his museum showed a traveling retrospective exhibition of Robert Mapplethorpe's photographs. This was despite the widely acknowledged artistic value of even the most shocking of the late photographer's works.

Prosecutors also used obscenity law in Florida in 1990 to bring criminal charges against the Miami rap group 2 Live Crew and a music store owner who sold their recordings. The fact that rap is one of the preeminent musical phenomena of the eighties and nineties, with record sales in the multimillions, didn't seem to matter—in fact, it probably only fueled the crusade. A federal court judge found 2 Live Crew's *As Nasty as They Wanna Be* album obscene, despite the testimony of experts that the music had serious artistic value, and of a local psychologist that it didn't appeal to prurient interests. An appeals court two years later overturned the obscenity ruling, but in the meantime, music store owner Charles Freeman had been convicted of obscenity and lost his business, based on the earlier federal court decision. (See Chapters 3 and 4 for more on this and other instances of music censorship.)

The parade of expert witnesses who populate these trials suggests another problem with current obscenity law—its elitism. Why should art or entertainment that doesn't command the admiration of judges, scholars, or other properly credentialed "experts" be banned? Why should those who like "lowbrow" entertainment be discriminated against? Judgments about "serious value" are subjective to begin with. As Supreme Court Justice Antonin Scalia has recognized, it's impossible "to come to an objective assessment of . . . literary or artistic value, there being many accomplished people who have found literature in Dada and art in the replication of a soup can."[15]

The obscenity exception to the First Amendment has no basis in history, logic, or constitutional law. Instead, it finds its origins in repressive social and cultural attitudes about sex—in the "moral panics" and culture wars of an earlier era. Obscenity law flourished in an era when the importance of talking about sex wasn't widely understood, or if it was understood, was considered highly subversive. The use of the law against birth control pioneers, writers about homosexuality, and advocates of women's sexual freedom, dramatizes the underlying ideological bias of obscenity prosecutions.

Those who would censor sexually oriented books and movies today sometimes argue that it's not a question of prudery about sex but of the degradation of women in erotic material. Whatever the validity of these arguments may be (see Chapter 7 for a discussion of the current debate among feminists over pornography), rest assured that those who have created and enforced obscenity laws throughout our history entertained no such egalitarian thoughts. They may have justified their actions with rhetoric about "protecting" women, but they certainly didn't intend to liberate them. Although even reactionary politicians today may speak in terms of the "objectification" or "degradation" of women in some pornographic works, their positions on reproductive rights, child care, and other issues of importance to women suggest that their antisex stance hardly flows from sensitivity to gender equality.

In addition to its lifelong ideological bias, obscenity law remains beset by the overwhelming defect of vagueness. It is as true today as ever that nobody knows just what the obscenity exception means. It's impossible for creators, retailers, or distributors to figure out which depictions or accounts of nudity or sexual activity predominantly appeal to a prurient interest in sex, are patently offensive to prevailing standards in any particular community, or lack serious literary, artistic, political, or scientific value. As a consequence, obscenity laws can't be enforced with any degree of fairness or consistency. They are inevitably subject to the whims and political ambitions of police or prosecutors, who in turn are often influenced by the attitudes and vociferousness of local "decency" brigades.

Justice Potter Stewart's famous quip in the 1968 case involving Louis Malle's film *The Lovers* is perhaps the most persuasive argument against obscenity laws: Stewart couldn't define obscenity, but, he wrote, "I know it when I see it." This is all very amusing, but it's a hell of a way to run a legal system.

The problems of vagueness and lack of predictability that plague all obscenity laws have only become more intense since the 1973 decision in *Miller*. Today, even the rural Maine and Mississippi of Chief Justice Burger's idyllic imaginings are diverse communities; their numerous citizens have countless different opinions on what is "patently offensive," "prurient," or lacking in "serious value."

In the twenty years since *Miller*, our nation has become freer in its discussions of sexuality and its access to materials about sex. Graphic details of cases involving sexual harassment and date rape are broadcast on television, as they should be: the cases are about sexual politics and women's rights in the deepest sense. Today we understand that talk about sex is political; it *is* an "essential part of the exposition of ideas," to borrow the language of the Supreme Court's *Chaplinsky* case.

Even highly charged speech with sexual content often has a political message. The four performance artists who sued the National Endowment for the Arts in 1990 because it denied their grant applications in response to political pressure are a case in point (see Chapter 6). The work of these artists—Karen Finley, Holly Hughes, Tim Miller, and John Fleck—is sexually explicit but far from pornographic. It needs to be explicit because its concerns are, in large part, the politics of sex: sexism, homophobia, sexual harassment, domestic violence, male dominance, the feminization of poverty, and the oppressiveness of traditional gender roles.

Apart from its political importance, information and entertainment about sex has therapeutic value. Today, whole bookstore sections are devoted to sex and marriage manuals with titles like *Women's Sexual Fantasies*, *The Art of Sexual Ecstasy*, *The Ultimate Sex Book*, and *How to Please a Woman Every Time*. Many psychologists recognize the value not only of this popular, mainstream type of sex manual, but of pornography—that is, material unabashedly intended for sexual stimulation. "Hard-core" pornography is readily available and, through the use of home video cassette players, widely enjoyed. According to the Adult Video Association, Americans rented more than 410 million adult videos in 1991.

Sex information is also a public health necessity. Health professionals acknowledge the value of, and dire need for, clear, explicit information, especially for teenagers, about condoms and how to use them. Because speech with graphic sexual content is now part of our daily lives, the vague strictures of obscenity law are more archaic and insupportable than ever.

Even when it comes to minors, parents differ in their child-rearing practices, their attitudes toward sexuality, and their views of what's appropriate for youths of different ages. Some parents and community members no doubt believe that all minors, even seventeen-year-olds, should be shielded from any material touching on sexuality or sexual relationships. Others feel that minors, especially teenagers, need accurate information about sex, both its mysteries and its sometimes-messy realities. In our diverse society, with its many differing attitudes toward child-rearing and sexuality, there is simply no common understanding of what is patently offensive or lacks serious value.

Now some individuals might view all this diversity, all this graphic frankness about sex, not as cause for celebration but as a sure harbinger of the decadence and decline of Western civilization. The point here, though, is not whether sexual openness and tolerance are good or bad, but whether, given current realities, terms like "patently offensive" and "prurient interest" can possibly have any discernible, predictable meaning.

The "prurient interest" test illustrates the heights of absurdity we have reached with obscenity law. According to a 1985 Supreme Court decision, "prurient" means only a "shameful" or "morbid" interest in sex. Works that arouse "normal" sexual appetites are not obscene. Thus, police, prosecutors, judges, and juries are supposed to distinguish between bad works that arouse "shameful" impulses, on the one hand, and materials that are okay because they inspire only healthy lust, on the other.

But what shameful as opposed to healthy means, when it comes to sexual fantasies, is anybody's guess. Are homosexual acts healthy or unhealthy? Bondage fantasies? An addiction to Harlequin romances? Does the standard change with locale—that is, can homosexuality be ruled healthy in San Francisco but unhealthy in San Jose? Surely it's strange to have a legal system in which judges and juries apply political tests to sexual fantasies by deciding what's healthy as opposed to unhealthy lust. Yet despite these anomalies, the Supreme Court's extension of First Amendment protection to books or movies arousing only "healthy" sexual desires is a positive step, because it recognizes the importance of sex, that "great and mysterious motive force in human life," as a serious subject of both political debate and artistic attention.

The obscenity exception to the First Amendment is today, as it has been throughout history, a ready vehicle for abuse by local authorities or pressure groups that want to impose their political or moral views on others by dictating what they can read, see, or hear. These officials and pressure groups justify their assaults on artistic freedom and individual choice with the rejoinder that they are not engaged in censorship because, as everyone knows, the First Amendment doesn't cover "obscenity."

Thus, the obscenity exception to the First Amendment remains a primary rhetorical as well as legal weapon in the hands of censors. It provides a field day for demagogues seeking to attack any material that touches on sex, from Judy Blume novels to avant-garde art, from classic paintings of nudes to pornography. They all can claim that, after all, obscenity is not protected by the First Amendment. The fact that no one can define obscenity is conveniently overlooked.

There's no excuse for perpetuating past mistakes. Ending the second-class citizenship of speech about sex would be a good start toward defeating censorship.

⚉ 2 ⚉

Movies: Censoring the Dream Factory

It is by the goodness of God in our country that we have those three unspeakably precious things: freedom of speech, freedom of conscience, and the prudence never to practice either of them.

—Mark Twain[1]

I N 1951 THE NEW YORK STATE BOARD OF REGENTS revoked a movie license it had previously granted for *The Miracle*, a film by the acclaimed Italian director Roberto Rossellini. The movie featured Anna Magnani as a peasant woman who suffered from delusions that she was the Virgin Mary. The Board of Regents had been under heavy pressure from the Roman Catholic Archdiocese to revoke the license on the ground that the film was "sacrilegious."

The U.S. Supreme Court overturned that decision the next year, pointing out that it was unconstitutional for government bodies to impose religious orthodoxies on movies or any other art. In the process, the Court ruled for the first time that films are a form of artistic expression protected by the First Amendment. But it didn't go so far as to invalidate the whole idea that government could establish censorship boards and require advance submission of movies for licensing.

American movie censorship is almost as old as Hollywood itself. In its mere century of existence, cinema has attained a popularity probably unmatched by any other art form. And with this popularity, this incredible ability to create or embellish popular myths and dreams, has come the drive to censor—to control the stories, ideas, words, and images shown with such powerful effect on the screen.

In the early days, censorship was legally easy to accomplish. Despite the artistic value of many early movies, the courts did not consider cinema to be a form of "speech" protected by the First Amendment, so there didn't seem to be any legal barrier to local governments creating agencies that reviewed films in advance, and decided which ones could be shown. The result was a dense growth of state and local censorship boards, each with its own procedures, personnel, attitudes, and standards of taste.

The Dream Factory Censors Itself

By the 1920s, the American movie industry was facing not only widespread government censorship but a bewildering hodgepodge of different, often conflicting standards and rules flowing from these various censorship boards. Films deemed acceptable in one city might be banned in another. Not only moral but political standards varied from place to place. Memphis, Tennessee, for example, prohibited *The Southerner* because the film was thought to reflect badly on the South, while Atlanta, Georgia, banned a work about a black doctor who passes for white because the censorship board thought the theme likely to inflame racial tensions.[2]

Films were censored for antiracist reasons as well. D. W. Griffith's 1915 silent film masterpiece, *Birth of a Nation*, was banned or altered in more than a dozen localities because of its white supremacist sympathies, racist stereotypes, and glorification of the Ku Klux Klan.[3] Yet this classic of film art is eminently worth seeing and studying, for its artistic brilliance as well as the historical light it sheds on America's violent history of racism.

Film producers faced not only an unmanageable burden of differing local censorship standards but increasing pressure from the Catholic Church's Legion of Decency, which berated the industry for its "low moral values." Hollywood responded, in the early 1930s, by creating a self-censorship scheme called the Hays Code, after former U.S. Postmaster General Will Hays, who was hired by the movie industry's trade association to head up the censorship office.

The Hays Code was created for two basic reasons: first, as a marketing device to persuade the public, especially powerful church groups, that the industry was not a promoter of immorality; and second, to standardize censorship so that movies would not be faced with a bewildering array of different standards imposed by different government licensing boards.

But in the interests of uniformity and morality, the Hays Office began to impose a kind of homogenizing banality on film artists. The code prohibited depictions of any nudity, interracial love, "excessive and lustful kissing," "adultery and illicit sex," or "dances suggesting or representing sexual actions." It banned any criticism of organized religion. Films dealing with crime or violence were also carefully controlled. They could not, for example, show law enforcement officers dying at the hands of criminals.

During the Hays Office's reign, industry censors and church representatives carefully reviewed scripts before films were made. The Protestant Film Office joined the Catholic Legion of Decency as a clearance agent. Producers and directors were told in advance what scenes or dialogue were unacceptable.

Thus, the Hays Office disapproved such shocking dialogue as Clark Gable's "Frankly, my dear, I don't give a damn," at the end of *Gone with the Wind.* It insisted on deleting a line from the classic 1931 Humphrey Bogart film, *The Maltese Falcon:* "Who is that dame wearin' my kimino?" It refused to approve a 1953 comedy called *The*

Moon is Blue because its characters mentioned words like "seduce" and "virgin."

In the case of *Gone With the Wind*, producer David O. Selznick put up a terrible fuss and eventually won the right to use the word "damn." *The Moon is Blue* wasn't so lucky, though, probably because its problem went deeper: The code office disliked *Moon* because it thought the film's entire approach to sex and seduction was too cavalier, thus violating the code rule that pictures not depict "low forms of sex relationship" as "the accepted or common thing." Though the film had respectable box-office success, even without a code seal of approval, the Hays Office maintained its hold over Hollywood for at least another decade.[4]

By the 1960s, though, the code was finally losing most of its starch. Increasingly, producers and directors were rebelling against the aesthetic and moral straitjacket it imposed. Less rigid attitudes about sex, more tolerance for diversity, more intellectual curiosity, and less willingness to defer to the dogmas and doctrines of the major churches, all contributed to the code's demise. In 1966, the Motion Picture Association of America (MPAA) replaced the code with the now-familiar G, PG, and R rating system. This system is hardly without its problems—and censorial effects—but compared to the Hays Code it is freedom incarnate.

The Hays Code Revived?

In early 1992 the large Roman Catholic Archdiocese of Los Angeles announced that its cardinal, Roger Mahony, was about to call for "a new motion picture and television Code." The cardinal was to make his pitch at a seminar scheduled for February 1, sponsored by the local Knights of Columbus and the "Hollywood Anti-Pornography Coalition." Two other speakers would be Ted Baehr of the Atlanta-based Christian Film and Television Commission, who would unveil a proposed model censorship code, and attorney Alan Sears, formerly of the Reagan administration's Meese Commission on Pornography (see Chapter 7).

"We are suffering a breakdown of morality, public health and public safety in America, especially among our youth," the archdiocese press release quoted Cardinal Mahony as saying in justification of this new call for movie censorship. "We, the people, have the right to decency on movie screens and on our public airwaves."

Underlying Cardinal Mahony's statement was the mistaken notion, so common among advocates of censorship, that the images, ideas, and stories shown on the big screen (or in any art form) actually *cause* the difficult, painful realities of modern society, instead of reflecting, confronting, protesting, or examining those realities. This scapegoating of art and entertainment has sometimes been described as "magical thinking." For those who subscribe to it, erasing, suppressing, or burying the ideas and images and stories will somehow erase the realities as well.

Cardinal Mahony's announcement elicited immediate and widespread reaction—from the media, the MPAA, various film writers' and directors' organizations, the American Civil Liberties Union, the Gay and Lesbian Alliance Against Defamation (GLAAD), and People for the American Way. Jack Valenti, head of the MPAA, protested that "a proliferation of rating systems would only confuse the very people we are trying to serve, the parents of America." GLAAD responded that the cardinal's proposal "would represent a throwback to the times when there was a 'legion of decency' in Hollywood—back to a time when all movies had to go before the Catholic Church for approval."

By the time of the February 1 seminar, Cardinal Mahony had backed away from demanding a new censorship scheme. He did not endorse the twenty-page model code distributed by fellow speaker Ted Baehr and his Christian Film and Television Commission. When asked what films he found objectionable, the Cardinal said he didn't go to very many movies, but that the Catholic Film Office had rated Martin Scorsese's recently released *Cape Fear* morally offensive "because it fosters revenge."

The example of *Cape Fear* may have been a revealing choice. It would take a single-minded inattention to the theme and structure of this thriller by a celebrated American director to interpret it as "fostering revenge." The film's lead character, a sociopath who pursues a meticulously planned and sadistic vendetta against his former defense attorney, is hardly presented as a model for emulation. But the Church might have been uncomfortable with *Cape Fear* for other reasons: its villainous lead character is a religious fanatic who views himself as the attorney's avenging angel. An overliteral interpretation might view the film as critical of religious belief.

The code proposal distributed by Ted Baehr at the February 1992 seminar began with a preface describing how a teenage girl who had recently viewed the hit movie *Pretty Woman* later got drunk and prostituted herself with a number of different men. Baehr, exhibiting a capacity for magical thinking at least equal to Cardinal Mahony's, declared that this sexy, entertaining fairy-tale film, a modern retelling of the Cinderella myth, was to blame for the young woman's behavior.

Baehr went on to note that in the Hays Code days, "the Church exerted a powerful influence in Hollywood through the Protestant Film Office and the Roman Catholic Legion of Decency." These church offices "insured that movies were wholesome and uplifting, that they did not denigrate the law or religion, and that they did not lower the moral standards of the audience." The Hays era so fondly recalled by Baehr also, of course, created a censorship system that strengthened and reinforced the control of powerful organized religious institutions over the information and ideas received by the American people. If any criticism of organized religion is banned, as it was under the Hays regime, people are certainly less likely to think for themselves about moral, spiritual, and even political matters.

In the days and weeks following the seminar, the Christian Film and Television Commission's mildly edited updating of the old Hays Code became the focus of public debate. Studying this twenty-page document not only illuminated much about America's culture wars, but provided a rare reminder of the moral/aesthetic standards that ruled American movies not very long ago.

The commission's proposed code began with a simple statement of principle, borrowed from its Hays Code model: "No movie shall be produced which will lower the moral standards of those who see it." The lengthy rules that followed were organized around particular subjects: crime, sex, vulgarity, obscenity, profanity, costume, dances, religion, and "national feelings."

The code section on crime barred movies from showing criminals "in such a way as to throw sympathy with the crime . . . or to inspire others with a desire for imitation." Methods of crime could not be "explicitly presented," and "illegal drug traffic" not portrayed in such a way as to "stimulate curiosity." There could be no "suggestion" of "excessive brutality," no "flaunting of weapons by gangsters or other criminals," and only minimal, if any, dialogue concerning guns. Suicide, "as a solution of problems occurring in the development of screen drama," was to be "discouraged as morally questionable and as bad theater—unless absolutely necessary for the development of the plot."

The code's section on sex began with the proposition that "the sanctity of the institution of marriage and the home shall be upheld." Adultery and "illicit sex," which the code acknowledged are "sometimes necessary plot material," could not be "explicitly treated or justified, or presented attractively." "Excessive and lustful kissing, lustful embraces, suggestive postures and gestures are not to be shown," and "passion should be treated in such manner as not to stimulate the baser emotions."

Ted Baehr's proposal also followed the Hays Code's detailed instructions on movie dialogue. Not only the common four-letter words, but "God," "Lord," "Jesus," and "Christ (unless used reverently)" were all prohibited, as were "fairy (in a vulgar sense); finger (the); Gawd, goose (in a vulgar sense); nuts (except when meaning crazy); pansy; slut (applied to a woman); and S.O.B." "Damn" and "hell" were banned except when used in a reverent, theologically proper context.

Ministers of religion could not be used as comic characters or villains. There could be no disrespectful treatment of the flag. "Repellent subjects" had to be "treated within the careful limits of good taste." This included "actual hangings or electrocutions," "inquisitions and torture," "surgical operations," and "the sale of women, or a woman selling her virtue."

The Baehr proposal did omit one important part of the old Hays Code: the ban on depictions of "miscegenation" (interracial love). Baehr and his Christian Commission obviously recognized that the virulent racism so entrenched in mid-century America was no longer acceptable. Other forms of prejudice, however, such as homophobia and the sexual double standard, remained.

Ted Baehr's proposed revival of the Hays Code may seem extreme, even silly. It's doubtful that most Americans today really want the doctrine of any church to decide when and how moviemakers can treat the subjects of sex, marriage, or crime or use the words "hell" and "damn." But the threat of a revised Hays Code in some form is real: the movie industry, like other branches of our vast entertainment empire, is driven by the twin desires for profit and public approval. When pressured, it will often yield.

The Recording Industry Association of America provided an example of this phenomenon in 1990 when it yielded to pressure to create a music labeling system (for more on this, see Chapter 4). The movie industry itself, back in 1947, yielded to pressures to institutionalize blacklisting of artists who were considered politically "unsafe." Unless consumers support artists and insist on artistic freedom, the entertainment industry is likely to yield again to pressures for internal censorship.

And the censorship is no less pervasive simply because it's "voluntary," that is, not imposed or required by the government— it's just that much more difficult to challenge legally, since the First Amendment applies only to government actions. Industry codes are hardly voluntary for the filmmakers, screenwriters, and other studio-employed artists whose fancies, fantasies, images, and sensibilities are routinely butchered under any censorship system that takes a narrowly literalistic view of complicated works of the imagination.

Beyond that, "voluntary" industry codes are inherently biased, both ideologically and morally, in favor of the dominant (or richest, or noisiest) religious, political, and cultural groups. Ted Baehr's advocacy of the old Hays Code dramatizes the problem. There is no consensus in contemporary American society about acceptable "moral standards," especially regarding sex and family matters. Not all Americans agree on certain "Christian" definitions of "evil" and "sin"—in fact, Christian denominations differ profoundly on these issues. Not everybody lives in a "traditional" two-parent nuclear family, and not everybody accepts the whole thick tapestry of cultural assumptions reflected in the concept of a "woman selling her virtue."

This isn't to say that "traditional" values, and the beliefs of large organized religious denominations, shouldn't be heard and respected. Those on the fundamentalist right who seek to censor ideas they deem insulting to their faith commonly fail to make this distinction. They're free to compete with other voices and other ideas—and they do so very effectively. But when they say that they're the victims of discrimination simply because those other voices can be heard as well, they're confusing the issue. It isn't discrimination to give everybody a chance to be heard.

All of the different values, traditions, and lifestyles that Americans choose ought to be respected: this is the fundamental meaning of the freedom of speech, free exercise of religion, and right to privacy guaranteed by our Constitution. Devout Christians who faithfully follow the teachings of the Roman Catholic Church or one of the fundamentalist Protestant denominations surely should not be forced to view movies not to their liking, or to send their children to view them. But neither should they impose their values on others who do not share their faith.

Government Censorship of Movies

The movie industry adopted the Hays Code in the 1930s in part to forestall what it saw as threatened government censorship. But the code system really didn't accomplish this purpose. As with any voluntary scheme devised in the hope of satiating those on the censorship bandwagon, the Hays Code, while perhaps satisfying some erstwhile censors, emboldened others to demand still more controls over the content of movies.

Thus, government licensing boards persisted well into the mid-twentieth century. The cities of Chicago, Detroit, Dallas, Memphis, Atlanta, Kansas City, Portland, Seattle, Houston, Denver, and Boston all had movie censorship boards—as did the states of New

York, Pennsylvania, Connecticut, Kansas, Maryland, Virginia, Ohio, and Rhode Island. These boards' refusals to license films not to their liking sparked the legal battles that eventually did away with most official movie censorship.

For example, a few years after the Supreme Court invalidated New York's revocation of a license for Roberto Rossellini's film, *The Miracle*, on the ground that states could not impose tests of religious orthodoxy on works of art, the Court rejected another New York ban, this time against a film version of D. H. Lawrence's sexually revolutionary novel, *Lady Chatterley's Lover* (which itself had been the subject of numerous censorship battles in Britain and the United States). The Court said that New York couldn't suppress the movie because of disagreement with its message that adultery can sometimes be proper behavior. That message, like advocacy of socialism or any other "ism," was free speech protected by the First Amendment. As in *The Miracle* case, though, the justices refused to go so far as to outlaw censorship boards entirely.

The assumption, rather, was that a government board *could* ban a movie because of obscenity. "Obscenity" was not protected by the First Amendment, and, of course, as far back as the Supreme Court's 1942 decision in *Chaplinsky* v. *New Hampshire*, obscenity was assumed not to imply any point of view on social or political issues.

In the sixties, the Supreme Court would greatly limit the power of state and local licensing agencies by requiring them to go to court promptly for a judicial determination of obscenity if they intended to prohibit a film from being shown in their area. Cities could no longer ban movies based on the personal predilections of the good citizens who were appointed to their licensing boards. Yet the Supreme Court still stopped short of obliterating the power of licensing boards, if backed up by courts, to ban films in advance of their showing—that is, to impose "prior restraints" on artistic expression. This has left room for today's censorship advocates to argue that film licensing agencies should be reinstated.

One such advocate is already familiar to us—freelance evangelist Ted Baehr. Before he appeared in Los Angeles in February 1992 to propose a revival of the Hays Code, Baehr and two colleagues—Thomas Radecki of the National Coalition on Television Violence and John Evans of Movie Morality Ministries—had created an organization that they called the National Association of Ratings Boards (NARB). Their plan was to circulate a model film censorship code, based on a system still operating in Dallas, Texas, and then persuade like-minded citizens around the country to lobby their local governments to adopt the code as a municipal ordinance.

Baehr's proposed NARB Film and Video Code required that every film or video to be distributed in a particular area would have to be submitted to a municipal board for classification as "suitable" or "unsuitable" for people under a certain age. Films would be considered "unsuitable" if they depicted "sexual conduct, nudity, defecation, or urination in a manner which is patently offensive to the average person applying contemporary community standards with respect to what is acceptable for viewing by young persons under specified ages." Films and videos would also be banned for young people if they depicted "the infliction of serious bodily injury" or serious damage to property, "without the express portrayal of significant adverse legal, physical, emotional, or societal consequences to the person who inflicts the injury, damage, or destruction." The proposed code also would ban minors from access to films or videos depicting "the use of illicit drugs, alcohol, or nicotine" without the "express portrayal" of "significant adverse consequences," if the use was "contrary to contemporary community legal, ethical, or moral standards." Despite all this contorted, legalistic language, Baehr's code turns on a series of subjective value judgments that, by requiring artists to show "significant adverse consequences," essentially reduces them to propagandists for the government.

Under the NARB scheme, exhibiting a film or renting a video to a minor without first submitting it for classification would be a crime. Additionally, of course, it would be illegal to show or rent a film labeled by the board as "unsuitable" to someone under the designated age. Finally, the board would classify films and videos with a variety of labels, such as L for profane language, N for nudity, D for drug, alcohol, or nicotine use, S for "sexual conduct or implicit sexual conduct or defecation or urination," V, V, and VVV for increasing levels of "infliction of serious bodily injury" or property damage, and P for "perverse person . . . or other seriously sexually degrading material." All movie ads would have to carry these government-required labels, even if the filmmakers and exhibitors disagreed with the way the government had characterized their work.

The NARB proposal falsely claimed that its model—the Dallas film classification board—had "repeatedly survived court tests." In fact, federal courts had declared the Dallas film board— the last remaining one of its kind—unconstitutional on at least three occasions. Three times Dallas reenacted its classification law with only minor changes. It wasn't until December 1992 that the Dallas censorship board was finally defanged. Before the December 1992 revisions, Dallas required all exhibitors or distributors to submit in advance for government rating all films to be shown in the city. In practice, the board classified all films rated R by the MPAA as "unsuitable," and therefore illegal to show to minors, even though most R-rated films would not violate state laws governing what is harmful or obscene as to minors. The Dallas board also occasionally rated PG-13 films "unsuitable." A 1992 example was the movie version of the popular musical *Serafina*, with Whoopi Goldberg; as in previous instances, though, the board changed its mind after the film's producers challenged its edict in court.

One movie theater in Dallas had long objected to the censorship board in principle and therefore refused to submit films for classification. In order to avoid criminal prosecution, the Inwood Theater simply advertised everything as "unsuitable" for kids. Thus, in June of 1992, the Inwood was showing the acclaimed Ismail Merchant–James Ivory film, *Howard's End*, with an "unsuitable" rating even though the toughest censor would have been hard put to identify anything harmful to minors in this elegant adaptation of the classic E. M. Forster novel.

In December 1992 the City of Dallas, under continuing fiscal and anticensorship pressures, finally repealed most of its archaic film-licensing ordinance. No longer would distributors have to publish government-mandated, derogatory warning labels; no longer would they be subject to criminal prosecution for admitting minors to a movie deemed morally unsuitable. All that remained was a requirement that companies submit films in advance; if the board decided a film was unsuitable for minors, it would advertise this opinion itself. It was unclear how seriously the city would try to enforce the advance submission requirement.

The year before Dallas finally shed its archaic film licensing board, Ted Baehr and other evangelists had launched their first major drive to replicate the Dallas model. They chose the neighboring city of Fort Worth, Texas, and, with their model code in tow, urged an ordinance expanding the Dallas system to regulate not only movies but videos that they considered unsuitable for minors. Intensive, sometimes emotional lobbying by both sides followed, but in the end it was a modest legal opinion by the Fort Worth city attorney that probably prevented passage of the measure.

Examining Texas state law, the Fort Worth attorney concluded that in Texas, regulation of "obscenity" and material "harmful to minors" were functions not of city, but state government. Municipalities could not go beyond the limits that the State of Texas had chosen to place on the exhibition of movies or, for that matter, the distribution of any other form of creative expression. The Fort Worth attorney also concluded that the proposed law was unconstitutionally vague and would violate the First Amendment.

Attempts like those in Fort Worth to extend film censorship from the movie theater to the video shop are probably inevitable. The video revolution has changed the form of America's entertainment rituals and lessened the role of the darkened theater as a place of communal enchantment. The ubiquity of home videos has also made policing the ratings system more difficult. Most movie theaters may subscribe to the MPAA code, but video stores tend to be a less predictable lot.

The arrival of the home video as a staple of contemporary life has also blurred the line between mainstream Hollywood entertainment (or arty foreign films) and what used to be considered sleazy, X-rated pornography. Consumers of "adult entertainment" need no longer frequent seedy theaters in the Times Squares of America; their corner suburban video store is more likely than not to have an erotica section. (See Chapter 3 for more on this phenomenon, and on the popularity of erotic videos among both women and men.)

The *Sex* book and video released by Madonna in late 1992 exemplifies the boundary-blurring that has occurred. This canny superstar consistently and deliberately teases the presumed lines between art, popular culture, and pornography. Indeed, Madonna isn't alone:

many less affluent and arguably more serious artists are also experimenting with line-crossing, using pornographic images to explore new territory in avant-garde and feminist art (see Chapter 7).

Other Dubious Moments in American Movie History

A chapter on movie censorship would not be complete without mention of the notorious Hollywood blacklist. Blacklisting is the practice of refusing to employ particular people because of their political beliefs or associations. The same industry that gave us the Hays Code in the thirties acquiesced in other sorts of political pressures in the late forties to establish that era's version of political correctness for writers, directors, producers, performers, and other workers in the movie industry.

It came at just about the time when government film-licensing boards were losing their grip, and even the industry's voluntary Hays Code was coming to be seen as a crusty, almost comical relic of archaic values. In October 1947 the U.S. House of Representatives Committee on Un-American Activities (popularly known as HUAC) held the first of what would be numerous hearings over the next decade to investigate alleged "communist subversion" throughout America. And what better place to start than Hollywood, with its glamour, its publicity potential, and its firm hold on America's fantasy life?

The Hollywood producers initially resisted HUAC's assault. MPAA president Eric Johnston boldly announced just weeks before the HUAC hearings that he would "never be party to anything as un-American as a blacklist." The first nineteen writers and directors to be subpoenaed had the support of a seemingly united movie industry as the hearings opened in Washington. But only ten of those nineteen ever got to testify. Their defiant refusal, based on free speech principles, to answer questions about their past or present political beliefs, or those of their friends, led to citations for contempt of Congress, and eventually to jail terms. In the glare of a media circus, the First Amendment abstractions that the "Hollywood Ten" tried to articulate couldn't compete with the smarmy insinuations of the HUAC questioners that any refusal to answer questions about past or present political beliefs was sure evidence of communist leanings.

Barely a month after the Hollywood Ten hearings, the movie producers turned about-face. After a meeting at New York's Waldorf Astoria Hotel, the Association of Motion Picture Producers announced that no "communist" or "member of any group or party which advocates the overthrow of the government" by force or "illegal" methods would work in Hollywood. Nor could any of the ten be employed until he had "purged himself"—and this meant "naming names" of others who had been involved in antifascist or left-wing activities in the thirties and forties. At least 250 actors, writers, producers, and directors were officially blacklisted from Hollywood as a result of the Waldorf statement. As the blacklist spread from movies to TV, radio, universities, unions, and government jobs, the toll was more than fifteen thousand people.[5]

Cases of mistaken identity abounded during the blacklist era; many people with no history of political activism were wrongly accused. A parasitic cottage industry of listmakers and purveyors developed to "help" studios and broadcasting companies decide who was "safe" enough to hire. For more than a decade, the integrity and artistic productivity of most of the American entertainment industry was held hostage to these self-appointed "clearance experts," and the politicians and demagogues who gave them clout. Not only the livelihoods but the very lives of talented film artists were devastated (several committed suicide). And the pall of orthodoxy that descended on the entertainment industry took its toll on creativity and political risk-taking in film and television content as well.

Today the blacklist in movies, radio, and television is almost universally condemned, but the impulse that created it is still with us. The rating and labeling schemes created by the movie and music industries, although focusing on undesirable subjects rather than people, are, like the blacklist, essentially attempts to placate pressure groups and politicians that want to impose ideological conformity on our naturally diverse and rambunctious American culture.

Ratings

The current MPAA rating system operates through a separate industry organization called the Classification and Rating Administration (CARA). The MPAA's president selects the chair of the CARA ratings board, and together they choose the "average American parents" who actually decide the ratings. He also chairs the ratings appeals board.

Though marketed as "consumer information," this rating system is also a form of censorship. To achieve the rating considered desirable by studios, creative artists routinely have to remove dialogue or even whole scenes from their work. American audiences rarely know what they're missing, except if they happen to catch the unexpurgated version of the movie playing in Europe or perhaps on a videocassette.

To be sure, in our economic system the studio that finances a movie controls its content. Film artists may be hard put to argue that they are being censored when their studio simply insists on certain changes—just as a reporter can't really complain if her editor dislikes her story, or an author, if his publisher insists on substantial editing as a condition for publication.

But the line between legitimate editorial control and illegitimate censorship begins to blur when it's not an individual production company but a powerful industrywide consortium that makes the ideological rules. It's the monopolistic nature of the MPAA system, the hold that the industry has over the economic means to market and distribute a film in the United States, that renders the rating scheme a form of censorship rather than simply an exercise in editorial or artistic judgment.

Where many different production companies are making independent editorial decisions, there's hope that diversity, and with it freedom, will prevail. Where an economic monolith controls the content and viewpoint of films, censorship is the predictable result. In the United States, "many theaters refuse to show an NC-17 film [a rating adopted in 1990 to replace the X], and many newspapers and radio and television stations will not carry advertising for one. Blockbuster Video, Kmart and Walmart, which account for more than half of the video sales in the United States, will not handle NC-17 titles."[6] (In 1992 a California anticensorship group organized weekly pickets in front of two Blockbuster stores in San Francisco in an effort—so far unavailing—to persuade the company to change its mind.) Though the line that separates an R movie from an NC-17 one is amorphous and subjective, the refusal to cut a film to satisfy the board's demands and achieve an R rating generally means restricting a film's exhibition opportunities to only about three hundred theaters nationwide.[7]

The inner workings of the movie rating system came to light during a lawsuit filed in 1990 by Miramax Films and the popular, often outrageous Spanish director Pedro Almodovar. They challenged the X rating that CARA had given to Almodovar's latest confection, *Tie Me Up, Tie Me Down*, a comedy based on the familiar fantasy but unlikely premise of a kidnap victim falling in love with her criminal abuser. Technically, the MPAA and CARA won the Miramax case. But in the course of his decision, Judge Charles Ramos expressed considerable disgust at the hypocrisy and arbitrariness of the rating system. He refused to second-guess the ratings board's decision, saying that he wouldn't "dignify the present system by rendering an opinion on so frivolous a standard as the wishes of the AAP" (that is, the "Average American Parent," the MPAA board's professed guideline). Judge Ramos went on to describe the rating system as "an effective form of censorship":

> The record reveals that films are produced and *negotiated* to fit the ratings. After an initial "X" rating of a film whole scenes or parts thereof are cut in order to fit within the "R" category. Contrary to our jurisprudence, which protects all forms of expression, the rating system censors serious films by the force of economic pressure.

Because Miramax had refused to delete two sexually explicit scenes, which the board required if the film was to avoid an X rating, *Tie Me Up* was distributed unrated. As Judge Ramos noted, the decision meant a substantial loss in potential revenue, as most theaters adhere to the National Association of Theater Owners, a cosponsor of the rating system, and thus will not show unrated films.

After the Miramax case, the MPAA changed the name for its X rating to the less damning NC-17. But even with its new moniker, this rating remains a stamp of economic doom, and few studios will risk it.

Even a star with the powerful draw of Madonna is hard put to fight the ratings. In late 1992 her steamy new movie, *Body of Evidence*, was cut to avoid the dreaded NC-17 rating. Because *Body of Evidence* was intended for mass marketing, not an art film crowd, the producer considered it "crucial that it be acceptable to exhibitors throughout the country."[8]

French director Louis Malle, by contrast, initially refused to make changes after his film, *Damage*, drew an NC-17 in late 1992. (A brief nude scene with Jeremy Irons and Juliette Binoche apparently upset the ratings board.) Malle reacted with astonishment: "It's unbelievable! Why does this country have such a strange taboo about nudity? They don't care about ice picks slashed into the chests of lovers like 'Basic Instinct.' . . . I find it sometimes weird here."[9]

Despite his indignation, Malle ultimately had to acquiesce in cuts to his film for the U.S. market. Critic Janet Maslin, reviewing *Damage*, noted that Malle's protests were reasonable, "since without its full sexual component this film is robbed of its best energy source."[10] Yet the willingness of directors like Malle and companies like Miramax to buck the system offers some hope that the monopolistic grip of the MPAA ratings may be loosening. The Hays Code was eventually defeated by producers who were willing to risk distributing their films without the code seal. If producers today become willing to take similar risks and more theaters become willing to show unrated films, the censorship power of the rating system can be defeated. The availability of videos—more difficult to regulate because distributed cheaply through so many small shops—may further erode the power of the ratings board to force homogenized standards and the mutilation of creative works.

This doesn't mean that the public will have no source of information about the content of movies. The MPAA's letter ratings offer precious little such information to begin with. Reviews, coming attractions, promotions, ads, and guides circulated by religious groups and others, too, are far more useful sources of information. And the economic stranglehold that forces filmmakers to censor their own work in deference to the MPAA's mythical "average American parent" will end.

But it will only happen if movie lovers make their voices heard and insist that censorship has no place in the dream factory.

❧ 3 ⓨ

Censorship by Suggestion:
The Problem of Government Threats

*People do not lightly disregard public officers' thinly veiled
threats to institute criminal proceedings against them if
they do not come around.*

—U.S. Supreme Court Justice William J. Brennan,
Bantam Books v. *Sullivan*[1]

WEST CHESTER, PENNSYLVANIA, SEPTEMBER 1991. Acting on a
complaint from the anti-pornography American Family Association, the district attorney in Chester County in eastern Pennsylvania has launched a campaign to get video store operators to
remove virtually all adult movie titles from their shelves. With
no advance warning and little publicity, D.A. James P.
MacElree 2d recently requested that police in the county visit all
video shops and furnish the owners with a list of more than 300
adult film titles. The retailers were asked to remove the cassettes
from circulation.

HIS BULLETIN FROM THE SEPTEMBER 14, 1991 ISSUE OF
Billboard magazine went on to report that if the store
owners refused the police demands, only *then* would the
police rent and watch the films "for possible prosecution on
obscenity grounds." The DA's technique of banning a whole cate-

gory of movies, without even viewing them, was a relatively new development in the censorship wars.

District Attorney MacElree's index of disapproved movies, which he had received from the American Family Association, included such titles as *All American Girls in Heat Part II*, *The Story of O*, *Caligula*, and *Beneath the Valley of the Ultra Vixens*. An indignant film scholar defended the last item, a creation of the much-admired high-camp director Russ Meyer. " 'Beneath the Valley of the Ultra Vixens' has absolutely no place on anybody's list of films that should not be shown or discussed," the scholar said. Russ Meyer, like Madonna, is an artist whose fusion of audacity, vulgarity, and social commentary has evidently inspired a loyal academic following.

Prosecutor MacElree's action was unusual only because of the length and specificity of his list. By 1991, it was common practice for police departments or DAs throughout the nation to short-circuit the legal process for deciding whether a work is obscene by merely suggesting, politely or not so politely, to local stores that they remove certain items from their stock.

LOWNDES COUNTY, GEORGIA, MARCH 1991—The Lowndes County Grand Jury met in secret and, according to a transcript of the meeting, viewed "certain video tapes rated NR, NC17, and X." The grand jurors, in the words of the transcript, agreed "that these tapes meet the criteria of the Georgia Obscenity Law." They thereupon directed Lowndes County Sheriff Robert Carter and the police chief of the City of Valdosta, Charlie Spray, to inform all local video stores of their instructions to remove "such obscene videotapes."

One small problem with this unusual procedure was that the grand jury didn't follow any recognized legal route for deciding the question of obscenity. A second error was that the grand jury's order was in effect a "prior restraint" on free speech—a government order silencing expression in advance of any judicial decision that it was illegal. Such prior restraints were common in the English legal system that the American Revolution and Bill of Rights so forcefully rejected. Today, they are considered the most constitutionally dubious of government actions suppressing speech.

A third minor oversight was that the Lowndes County Grand Jury, as well as Sheriff Carter and Police Chief Spray, failed to inform the local video stores what movies they thought were obscene. This oversight may have been intentional, though: like government officials in other localities, the Lowndes County grand jurors apparently hoped to wipe out not merely specific titles but a whole category of entertainment.

Accordingly, the letters that the video stores received from Chief Spray and Sheriff Carter simply informed them that the Lowndes County Grand Jury wished them to be aware of the state obscenity law, and of the fact that "on or about April 15, 1991," they would "take such action as may be necessary to comply with the mandate of the grand jury."

Unlike many retailers in small and medium-sized communities who are faced with letters, warnings, threats, or demands like those of Messrs. Spray and Carter, and who quietly acquiesce, the video stores in Valdosta consulted a lawyer and decided to pool their resources to challenge the legality of the grand jury's order. This was an excellent start toward fighting the growing tendency toward imposing informal schemes of censorship through letters and warnings. But what happened afterward was even more instructive about the subtle ways that censorship can happen.

The video stores went to court requesting a preliminary injunction—an order to the sheriff and police chief to withdraw their threats. Faced with this request, Judge Wilbur D. Owens, Jr., decided to give everybody a friendly talking-to. He pointed out to Sheriff Carter that the grand jury's procedure was highly improper, and thereby secured an agreement that such letters would not be sent again. The judge saw no need for a court order.

Of course, by this time, the damage had been done. Not wishing to invite criminal prosecution, the stores had withdrawn all adult videos pending the court hearing. Now, even after the judge's agreement that the local officers had acted unlawfully, the stores were intimidated—and short of money to continue the court fight. Discretion being the better part of valor for most businesses, the owners were reluctant to invite prosecution. Censorship was quietly accomplished in Valdosta *despite* the illegality of the government's behavior.

BUTLER COUNTY, OHIO, JUNE 1991—The Butler County sheriff met with local video store owners to go over their inventories and agree on which films should be removed from circulation. The sheriff promised not to bring any prosecutions until the negotiations were concluded. As in West Chester, Pennsylvania, the sheriff's list of forbidden products was based on titles, not actual review of film contents. One store was told to remove *Doing it Debbie's Way*, which turned out to be a Debbie Reynolds exercise tape.

The Butler County stores sought legal counsel, but preferred not to sue. Lawsuits are not only expensive but lengthy, uncertain, and confrontational—and they tend not to endear you to the local authorities whose good graces you need to operate a business.

Negotiation was also to the government's advantage. Why risk expensive, difficult, and film-by-film obscenity prosecutions, replete with expert witnesses, when you can accomplish a far broader goal—removal of a whole category of films—through a combination of threats and "friendly" suggestions?

The negotiations produced an informal agreement under which *some* adult tapes would be permitted—but not the really "bad" ones. What is really bad depends, of course, on one's particular values and attitudes about sexuality. In some places, depictions of sadomasochistic fantasies are "really bad," while in others it's homosexuality. When a similar deal was cut in 1992 between prosecutors and video stores in a North Carolina county, it was the gay-oriented videos that had to go.

NORWOOD, MASSACHUSETTS, MAY 1991—There was a very different outcome when the police in this suburb of Boston began threatening video stores. As in Valdosta, West Chester, and Butler County, the several general-purpose video stores in town had maintained adult sections for years without incident. Now, at the behest of one local complainant, Police Chief George DiBlasi visited all the stores and claimed to be *shocked* to discover erotic material freely purveyed in his community. Within the next few days, he sent police officers to each store to advise the owners to remove their adult or X-rated videos. All but one of the entrepreneurs obliged.

The one dissenter was Daina Laverty, owner of Video Haven. As was well-known in the video business, the adult category by 1991 accounted for 15–30 percent of sales—a margin that Daina Laverty felt she could not comfortably sacrifice. She asked the police whether she didn't have a First Amendment right to sell or rent these tapes. They responded by supplying her with a photocopy of the Massachusetts obscenity law. Like most such laws, this one simply repeats the three-part definition of obscenity found in *Miller* v. *California*, and thus is not too helpful in specifying what's legal and what isn't (see Chapter 1 for the *Miller* definition).

Laverty and the Norwood Police Department locked horns for the next several weeks. The town wasn't particularly eager to prosecute; indeed, it was not clear that the county DA's office would view this as a priority criminal case. On Laverty's side, she certainly didn't want to be prosecuted, but nor did she relish the idea of giving up her livelihood. If the police had pointed to one or two tapes they found objectionable, she might have acquiesced; but their sweeping demand to remove all adult material, without having viewed any of it, seemed a bit much.

Laverty contacted the Free Speech Legal Defense Fund, an organization that the adult video industry had formed that year to help defend itself against sharply mounting attacks from the U.S. Department of Justice (see Chapter 6 for more on the dubious activities of Justice's antipornography squad). The fund called the ACLU's Arts Censorship Project, which in turn consulted with the Civil Liberties Union of Massachusetts. The ACLU groups agreed to represent Laverty and two other video stores in a legal challenge to the police department's conduct. This would be a civil suit, not a criminal prosecution. As in Valdosta, Georgia, the Norwood stores would be asking the court for an injunction prohibiting the town officials from making any further threats.

But before they had a chance to file the suit, Laverty was arrested and charged with three counts of distributing obscenity. The tapes in question were called *Fuck 'n A, Backdoor Romance*, and *The Adventures of Dick Black, the Black Dick*. The police had evidently chosen what they thought would be most likely to offend a local jury—anal and interracial sex.

Now a problem of court procedure arose. It was pretty clear that the charges against Laverty were brought in retaliation for her exercise of constitutional rights: she had refused to acquiesce in the police demands, whereas the other stores, which had been selling the same or similar material, caved in to the demands and weren't prosecuted. Yet it might be hard to prove this retaliatory motivation, and even harder to persuade a judge in the civil suit actually to order the dismissal of criminal charges. Courts in civil cases are notoriously reluctant to interfere in criminal ones. Laverty might end up with a criminal record even if she won the civil suit.

As the civil case seeking the injunction progressed through the discovery phase (exchange of information), an interesting transformation occurred. The police department now claimed that its officers had never told anybody to get rid of adult or X-rated videos. All they had done was politely drop off a copy of the state obscenity law and warn the stores to make sure they didn't have any "obscene" material in stock.

The reasons for this new line were readily apparent. Whereas adult or X-rated videos are presumed to have First Amendment protection unless and until a court rules otherwise with respect to a specific film, obscenity laws do exist and have been held constitutional. Thus, it's up to store owners, producers, and distributors to try to figure out whether anything they have in stock *might* offend community standards, appeal to prurient interests, or lack serious value (the three parts of the obscenity test). If all the Norwood police had done was to alert video store owners about the existence of the state obscenity law, their conduct probably wouldn't be ruled unconstitutional. The only problem was that this *wasn't* what the Norwood police had done, and the plaintiff stores had witnesses to prove it.

Laverty's case was settled midway through the trial, and on terms very favorable to the plaintiffs. Under the agreement, the police would make no further threats to the stores, and the town would seek dismissal of the criminal charges against Daina Laverty. Most important, if the police thought a *particular* video was obscene, they would start a civil—not criminal— proceeding to find out if they were right.

Massachusetts law already mandates this civil proceeding for books and magazines, and it makes sense. Since the obscenity laws are so vague, nobody should have to face criminal prosecution without at least being on notice that the work they are distributing actually *has* been ruled obscene.

In Norwood, Massachusetts, as a result of the Laverty case, people may buy or rent whatever videos they choose—and those who prefer something a bit more highbrow than *Debbie Does Dallas* are free to ignore the adult section of the video store.

A Cautionary Tale: The Rhode Island Commission to Encourage Morality in Youth

Today, adult videos and rap music tend to be the targets of censorship by suggestion, and blamed for all manner of social ills. In the fifties the concern was "juvenile delinquency," and crime stories and comic books were identified as likely culprits.

Thus, in 1956 the State of Rhode Island created a Commission to Encourage Morality in Youth, with a mandate to "educate the public concerning any book, picture, pamphlet, ballad, printed paper or other thing containing obscene, indecent or impure language, or manifestly tending to the corruption of the youth." The commission developed the practice of notifying distributors that it considered certain books or magazines in their stock to be objectionable, to thank them in advance for their "cooperation," and then to remind them of the commission's duty to recommend cases to the attorney general for prosecution. A police officer usually visited the distributor shortly after the notice was sent to see what action had been taken.

One problem with this scheme was that those who were most directly affected—the publishers and authors of the works in question—were not notified and had no way to object. Distributors, handling thousands of titles, naturally had less interest in the First Amendment rights of particular authors or publishers and more in getting on peacefully with the local authorities. Consequently, it was a publisher, Bantam Books, that brought a legal challenge to the Rhode Island system.

The case eventually made its way to the Supreme Court, which ruled that the Rhode Island commission had created an unconstitutional, if informal, system of government censorship through prior restraints. Rejecting the state's protest that it was merely offering "advice" that the distributors were free to ignore, the Court said that it intended "to look through forms to the substance," and that "compliance with the Commission's directives was not voluntary": "It would be naive to credit the State's assertion that these blacklists are in the nature of mere legal advice when they plainly serve as instruments of regulation independent of the laws against obscenity."[2]

In *Bantam Books* v. *Sullivan* the Supreme Court did note that not all "private consultation between law enforcement officers and distributors" would be unconstitutional. "Where such consultation is genuinely undertaken with the purpose of aiding the distributor to comply with [the] laws and avoid prosecution under them, it need not retard the full enjoyment of First Amendment freedoms." However, the Court did not illuminate how the line between threats and "consultation" was to be drawn.

The difficulty of locating that line was demonstrated in 1986 when the Attorney General's Commission on Pornography, established by Reagan administration Attorney General Edwin Meese, sent letters to twenty-three companies, owners of convenience store chains such as 7-11, informing them that they were considered distributors of "pornography" and would be so listed in the commission's final report unless they contested the accusation. The companies had been identified by Donald Wildmon, leader of an up-and-coming religious right pressure group called the National Federation of Decency (its name was later changed to the less puritanical-sounding American Family Association). The Meese Commission's not-so-hidden message was to get rid of *Playboy*, *Penthouse*, and similar soft-core erotic magazines.

Playboy and *Penthouse* went to court, arguing that, as in *Bantam Books*, the Meese Commision had made threats for the clear purpose of accomplishing censorship. A federal judge found as a preliminary matter that the commission had probably acted unconstitutionally, and ordered a retraction of the letter. But meanwhile, the Southland Corporation, owner of 7-11, had agreed to stop selling *Playboy* and its imitators.

Later, the courts refused to award money damages as compensation for *Playboy*'s and *Penthouse*'s loss of sales. They said that the Meese Commission's behavior was sufficiently different from the Rhode Island commission in *Bantam Books*, so it really wouldn't be fair to order the people who were responsible for the letter to pay damages. The federal court of appeals opined:

> In our case, the Advisory Commission had no . . . tie to prosecutorial power nor authority to censor publications. The letter it sent contained no threat to prosecute, nor intimation of intent to proscribe the distribution of the publications. Penthouse argues that since the letter was written on Justice Department stationery, used the term "allegations," and contained an instruction to contact an attorney for further information, recipients would reasonably think they were threatened with prosecution. . . . It may well be that the Commission came close to implying more authority than it either had or explicitly claimed. Nevertheless, . . . we do not believe that the Commission ever threatened to use the coercive power of the state against the recipients of the letter.[3]

This court's refusal to recognize the coercive effect of the Meese Commission's techniques (official stationery, legal language, instructions to contact an attorney) betrayed a kind of formalism that contrasts sharply with the Supreme Court's insistence in *Bantam Books* on "looking through forms to the substance." Certainly, this excerpt from the *Penthouse* decision ignored the likely effect of letters like that of the Meese Commission, whether or not they are technically threats.

The ruling that *Playboy* and *Penthouse* couldn't collect damages was a setback to efforts to stop censorship by government suggestion. Once done, censorship through threats can rarely be undone, even if a court later rules that the government acted illegally. We need other, meaningful remedies for the informal book, movie, and music banning that goes on. One such remedy—traditionally recognized for the violation of constitutional rights—is money damages. Knowing you may be liable for damages if you violate somebody's rights is a pretty good deterrent to bad conduct. At least, that's the theory of our civil law system.

When the courts set up rules that make it extraordinarily difficult to win money damages from government officers, then the system isn't doing its job. And because local retailers and distributors are so vulnerable, because there aren't enough anticensorship lawyers to go around, and because lawsuits are long and costly, the result is that threats continue to be one of the most pervasive yet least recognized forms of censorship.

People might reasonably ask what the big problem is with censorship by suggestion. After all, as long as obscenity and "harmful to minors" laws exist, many distributors and retailers will want to know in advance when they are likely to run into trouble. Police and prosecutors argue, as they did in the Norwood, Massachusetts, case, that most people would rather be warned when they're jaywalking and given a second chance than arrested and hauled to the hoosegow.

The answer is that art and entertainment are different from jaywalking. When officers of the law give warnings against books, magazines, movies, videos, music, or works of visual art, they are attempting to suppress information, works of the imagination and intellect—and to do so based on personal attitudes or tastes, without the benefit of any fair procedure. And because it happens quietly, because artists may never even know about it, this is censorship of a most insidious kind—even when the cops are friendly and polite.

The Rhode Island Commission Revisited: Threats to Popular Music

What happened in West Chester, Butler County, Valdosta, and Norwood, and what happened to *Playboy* and *Penthouse*, are typical scenarios that continue to be played out in countless cities and towns across America. And the targets of censorship by suggestion are expanding, from films and books to music.

Increasingly, local authorities are asking, advising, or ordering music stores not to carry albums with sexually explicit or politically controversial lyrics. Some are urging removal of rap music with radical black power or antipolice messages; others seek to get rid of all albums with the music industry's supposedly voluntary "Parental Advisory/Explicit Lyrics" label. This label, affixed to certain albums by their production companies, has no uniform meaning or legal significance, and certainly doesn't establish that the music is obscene or harmful to minors within the legal meaning of those terms. (See Chapter 4 for more on the origins of the advisory label and on the past and present wars against popular music.) Yet stores are agreeing not to carry labeled recordings, or at least not to sell them to teenagers. Music stores, like video stores, cave into these demands by local authorities because they don't want to risk criminal prosecution and they do want to maintain a good image in the community.

Not surprisingly, the most frequent targets of the informal threat system of music censorship have been rap and rock. In 1990 *Bantam Books* came to Florida.

Sheriff Nick Navarro of Florida's Broward County had taken a strong dislike to the creative offerings of a local rap group, 2 Live Crew. Formed by Luther Campbell, a native of Miami's Liberty City ghetto, 2 Live Crew specialized in the "Miami bass" style of hip hop music. Hip hop combines dance rhythms, witty, provocative verbal "raps," and a variety of stylistic devices like "call and response," boasting, "doing the dozens" (that is, trading insults), and "sampling" (digitally lifting quotes and riffs from other musicians).

By the late 1980s, hip hop and rap music were sweeping the country, gaining popularity well beyond their inner-city roots. Their most prominent practitioners, groups like Public Enemy or N.W.A. (Niggas With Attitude), expressed black pride and anger about police abuse, poverty, and racial injustice, in driving rhythms and occasionally apocalyptic poetry.

Like the more political rappers, Luther Campbell and his crew produced music with a fast, infectiously danceable beat, rhythmic lyrics, alliterations, puns, and other techniques typical of rap. But unlike groups such as Public Enemy, 2 Live Crew's raps focused almost exclusively, and many would say misogynistically, on sex. 2 Live Crew's musicians celebrated their male phallic enthusiasm in blunt, unambiguous language.

Sheriff Navarro, presumably preferring a more subtle approach to sexual matters, submitted the group's recent album, appropriately named *As Nasty as They Wanna Be*, to a local judge for a determination as to whether it violated Florida's obscenity law. This was not a trial in any sense; neither Luther Campbell nor any music store selling his album was notified of the procedure. Instead, Judge Mel Grossman of Broward County Circuit Court reviewed the tape and the lyrics that Navarro had transcribed from six of the eighteen songs on the album, and in March 1990 issued a "probable cause" ruling that the album, taken as a whole, was obscene and therefore illegal under Florida law.

Sheriff Navarro's office now distributed this "probable cause" order countywide. Deputies visited between fifteen and twenty stores and told the managers to stop selling the album: further sales would result in arrest. Within days, all retail stores in Broward County had stopped selling it. Those stores not actually visited by a deputy sheriff pulled the album after hearing TV and radio reports.

2 Live Crew's label, Skyywalker Records, went to court to try and stop the sheriff's broad-ranging censorship campaign. Federal Judge José Gonzalez, who was so hostile to the music itself that he later ruled it legally obscene, nevertheless recognized the dangers inherent in Sheriff Navarro's letter-and-visit approach. A probable cause order is far from a real determination of obscenity, made after a full judicial hearing in which all sides—including experts on the subjects of prurient interest and serious value—can be heard. Sheriff Navarro's suppression of *As Nasty as They Wanna Be*, like the Rhode Island commission's antics thirty years before, amounted to a prior restraint on free speech, in violation of the First Amendment. Said Judge Gonzalez: "Individuals confronted with the threat of arrest by law enforcement officers and presented with a court's order can be expected to do as they are told."[4]

Nick Navarro's crusade against rap music did not abate; the conflict now moved from threats to criminal prosecutions. Hip hop musicians were pushing some powerful buttons, both racial and sexual. As the next chapter recounts, music censorship remains one of the hottest fronts in the American culture war.

⊘ **4** ⊘

"The Devil's Music":
The Oddity of Warning Labels on Art

There should be warning labels on politicians.

—Derek Smalls, bass player for Spinal Tap

Miami Bass and "Dirty Rap"

POPULAR MUSIC HAS BEEN A RELATIVE NEWCOMER TO THE world of obscenity law. But in 1988 prosecutors in the town of Alexander City, Alabama, charged Tommy Hammond, the owner of Take Home the Hits music store, with the crime of obscenity for selling an earlier album called *Move Somethin'*, by the Miami rappers 2 Live Crew. After a swift hearing, Hammond was convicted by a municipal judge. He appealed, claiming his right to a new trial before a jury, and found new counsel with the ACLU of Alabama.

When Hammond's case reached that Alabama jury almost two years later, *Newsday* music critic John Leland and Columbia University political science professor Carlton Long testified as experts for the defense, explaining the social origins and artistic value of rap music. Long traced conventions in African American culture and music dating from the era of slavery. He explained the genesis of techniques like call and response, boasting, and doing the dozens. Hammond was acquitted.

The Hammond case was barely concluded in early 1990 when Florida's Sheriff Nick Navarro, perhaps inspired by the events in Alabama, began his own campaign against 2 Live Crew by procuring a "probable cause" order that the group's *As Nasty as They Wanna Be* album was obscene. Skyywalker Record's subsequent civil lawsuit challenged Navarro's tactics and also sought a federal court ruling that the music was not in fact obscene.

In the trial that followed, music critic John Leland and political science professor Carlton Long once again traveled south to testify in support of Miami rap, but evidently Florida Judge José Gonzalez was not as impressed with their expert testimony as the Alabama jury had been in the Hammond case. The judge dismissed Professor Long's testimony that *As Nasty as They Wanna Be* had political value by remarking that just because the group's music reflected their "heritage as black Americans," this did not "convert whatever they say, or sing, into political speech."[1] Nor was the judge impressed with Long's description of the song "Dick Almighty" as "an example of the literary device of personification." (The song certainly is a classic of comic exaggeration, though: Judge Gonzalez evidently didn't appreciate the bawdy humor and parody of excessive machismo in such lines as, "it's fifteen inches long, eight inches thick / last name Almighty, first name is Dick.")

Judge Gonzalez also paid little heed to a Miami psychologist's testimony that the album didn't appeal to the prurient interest of the average South Florida adult. Dr. Mary Haber based her opinion on years of clinical experience with a wide range of relatively normal Floridians. She explained that men are primarily aroused by pictures; women by written pornography; but neither by musical lyrics. Since the prurient interest test required sexual arousal, the album failed miserably.

Judge Gonzalez also minimized the importance of critic John Leland's testimony about rap's musical language, which involves borrowing and lifting riffs from other musical forms (such as jazz, blues, soul, and rock), and blending textures—for example, bits of speech with bass rhythms, horn or guitar figures, and electronic sounds. Leland testified,

> In the past, you would look at a piece of music as being built out of notes and chords and tones. Those would be the basic building blocks. . . . Hip hop throws that out, and says the basic building blocks are little chips of other records, and we'll create an original work of music; not starting with notes and chords and tones, but we'll create them from other records.

Finally, Judge Gonzalez rejected Skyywalker Records' argument that the album had serious value as satire and comedy. *He* did not think it was funny, although he acknowledged that "the meaning of music is subjective and subject only to the limits of the listener's imagination." In his opinion, the album consisted almost entirely of "rhythm and explicit sexual lyrics which are utterly without any redeeming social value."[2]

Ironically, later in 1990 a South Florida jury acquitted the four members of 2 Live Crew of obscenity charges, based on a live performance of four songs from their infamous album ("Me So Horny," "Put Her in the Buck," "C'mon Babe," and "The Fuck Shop"). Barely a month earlier, African American record store owner Charles Freeman, who had defied Judge Gonzalez' ruling, had been convicted of obscenity by an all-white jury.

It took nearly two years for a federal court of appeals to reverse Judge Gonzalez in a brief but telling opinion. Picking up on a theme from the trial, the three appellate judges said, "we tend to agree . . . that because music possesses inherent artistic value, no work of music alone may be declared obscene."[3] The court found that the government had simply failed to meet its legal burden of proving that *As Nasty as They Wanna Be* met all three parts of the *Miller* v. *California* obscenity test. Judge Gonzalez, the court ruled, couldn't rely on his own subjective opinions in the face of unrebutted evidence from experts about the album's artistic value. The government had done nothing at trial to contradict Professor Long's testimony that the album contained statements of political significance—for example, commentaries on men who don't help support their children—or examples of literary conventions such as alliteration, allusion, metaphor, and rhyme.

Is Rock 'n' Roll Worse Than Ever?
The Campaign for Labeling

Before the 2 Live Crew cases, obscenity prosecutions against music had been virtually unheard of. But that didn't mean that music wasn't the target of censorship. Throughout the twentieth century, this most visceral and hypnotic of art forms has been attacked for salacious lyrics, hip-grinding rhythms, or politically provocative messages.

Jazz and blues, the forerunners of rock music, were creations of African American culture. Both were attacked as "jungle rhythms" and "the devil's music," in rhetoric that was drenched in the ugly racism of early- and mid-twentieth-century America. Jazz innovator Count Basie recalled "particularly one comment in the 1930s, which said jam sessions, jitterbugs, and cannibalistic rhythm orgies are wooing our youth along the primrose path to hell.' "[4]

Racism and fear of race-mixing became particularly pronounced in the fifties as rhythm and blues evolved into rock 'n' roll, attracting increasing numbers of white fans and performers. Alabama's White Citizens Council charged in 1956 that rock 'n' roll—"'the basic, heavy-beat music of the Negroes'—appealed to 'the base in man, brings out animalism and vulgarity,' and, most important, formed a 'plot to mongrelize America.'"[5] At the famous Senate hearings on "payola" in 1958, author Vance Packard cautioned that rock 'n' roll stirred "'the animal instinct in modern teenagers' by its 'raw savage tone.'" The Houston, Texas, Juvenile Delinquency and Crime Commission condemned thirty songs that it considered obscene, all of them by black artists, including the Drifters' "Honey Love" and Ray Charles's "I Got a Woman." An April 1956 issue of *Variety* blamed rock music for "a staggering wave of juvenile violence and mayhem," while the Pennsylvania Chief of Police Association asserted that rock provided "an incentive to teenage unrest."[6]

Sex, racial integration, radical politics, flirtation with demonic themes, drug experiences—all were cited in attacks on popular music in the fifties and sixties. The powerful TV variety show host Ed Sullivan called the hip-swiveling Elvis Presley "unfit for a family audience," but reversed his opinion a few years later and invited Presley to appear on the show. (Elvis was, however, filmed only from the waist up.) The TV networks blacklisted folk singers like Woody Guthrie, Pete Seeger, and the Weavers because they were viewed as radicals who sang of racial injustice, poverty, imperialism, and other politically unacceptable themes. Guthrie's spiritual heir Bob Dylan refused to perform on Ed Sullivan after being told he could not sing his "Talkin' John Birch Society Blues." The Rolling Stones were attacked for "pornographic lyrics"; when they appeared on Ed Sullivan in 1965, words from their hit song "Satisfaction" were beeped out. Two years later, "Let's Spend the Night Together" had to be sanitized to "Let's Spend Some Time Together" before it could be aired.[7]

In the seventies, punk rock inspired new censorship efforts. The Sex Pistols, a band that loudly expressed the rebellious anger of

unemployed British youth, was banned by almost every munici-
pality in Britain. Their second single, "God Save the Queen," could
not be broadcast on British radio.[8] Its lyrics included:

> God save the Queen, a fascist regime
> It made you a moron, a potential H-bomb
> God save the Queen, she ain't no human being
> And there's no future in England's dream.

How quickly the demons and scapegoats of yesterday become
the cultural icons of today. Just as painters who, in their lifetimes,
were attacked for sexual or political unacceptability are now lion-
ized in our leading museums, so pop musicians like Elvis, once vilified for sexual degeneracy, are now immortalized on U.S. postage
stamps.

The more recent troubles of popular music, and its role in
America's culture war, go back at least to 1985, when a group of
Washington political wives—Elizabeth "Tipper" Gore most prominent among them—began an organization, the Parents Music
Resource Center (PMRC), whose goal was to focus public attention, and outrage if possible, on the subject matter and lyrical
explicitness of rock 'n' roll.

The PMRC was particularly concerned about heavy-metal rock
music with lyrics involving sex, drugs, alcohol, suicide, violence, or
the occult. They targeted rock groups like Twisted Sister, Iron
Maiden, Black Sabbath, and Judas Priest. These heavy-metal musicians had emerged from the combined rock and "electric blues"
styles pioneered by such artists as Jimi Hendrix in the late sixties.
Hendrix once explained: "Lots of young people now feel they're not
getting a fair deal. So they revert to something loud, harsh, almost
verging on violence; if they didn't go to a concert, they might be
going to a riot."[9]

Like rappers in the eighties and nineties, Hendrix and his heavy-metal successors reflected and articulated, but did not cause, youthful alienation, aggression, and occasional fascination with the demonic in human experience and imagination. "I don't profess to be a messiah to slum people," said Black Sabbath vocalist Ozzy Osbourne, "but I was a back-street kid, and that little demon is still in there, shoving the hot coal in. The aggression I play is the aggression I know."[10]

Tipper Gore explained that she first became concerned about rock music while overhearing the song, "Darling Nikki," by the pop megastar Prince. "Darling Nikki" refers to masturbation, a topic not unknown to most teenagers. Yet Gore and the PMRC were sufficiently alarmed to demand that music companies affix warning labels to recordings. Under the system proposed by PMRC, V would stand for violence; X for sexually explicit lyrics; O for occult, and so on. Presumably these labels would alert parents to the content of what their youngsters were hearing.

Because these Washington political wives had powerful connections and lots of access to the media, their complaints were taken seriously. In September 1985 the Senate Commerce Committee (of which Tipper Gore's spouse, Al, was a member) convened hearings to investigate the subversive tendencies of rock music. The hearings became a kind of media circus in which Senator Ernest Hollings attacked rock as "outrageous filth" that he would ban completely if he could. Sixties musical legend Frank Zappa described the perils of labeling, recounting how one music store had labeled his album, *Jazz from Hell*—even though it was entirely instrumental.

Pop singer John Denver, another opponent of labeling, told how some radio stations had refused to broadcast his song, "Rocky Mountain High," mistakenly thinking it was about drugs. Denver explained that the high he sang of came from "a moonless and cloudless night where there are so many stars that you cast a shadow."[11] Denver's message was one that applies to all the arts: you can't be overliteral about the ideas that you think an artist is expressing.

Tipper Gore later termed these 1985 Senate hearings a mistake. The hearings, she said, "gave the misperception that there was censorship involved."[12]

Yet even before the Senate hearings ended, the Recording Industry Association of America (RIAA) acquiesced in the PMRC's demands and announced that it would encourage its member companies to put "explicit lyrics" warning labels on their raunchier items, though not the detailed alphabet soup of designations that PMRC had demanded.

The women who began PMRC shouldn't have been so shocked to discover that sex, violence, getting high, suicide, and the supernatural were common themes in rock music. These are some of the perennial subjects of interest to teenagers—in fact, they're familiar themes in the arts throughout history.

The human imagination has long been fascinated by tales of violent crime or adventure, or of the occult and supernatural. Shakespeare's *Macbeth* and *The Tempest*, not to mention the innumerable literary and operatic retellings of the Faust legend or the bone-chilling stories of Edgar Allan Poe, are just a few examples of the pervasiveness of themes like occultism, witchcraft, black magic, and the supernatural in literature and the other arts. Paintings by the Spanish master Francisco de Goya, to take just one instance from the visual arts, are drenched in occultism.

It would be hard to tell where, in the worldview of the PMRC, references to legitimate religious experience ended and illegitimate "occultism" began. The devil has always been a major character in

Western art and literature. Who's to decide which works parents should be "warned" about?

Suicide has likewise been a subject of considerable fascination in the arts. Poor Hamlet, barely more than a teenager himself, was obsessed with it, as generations of high school students are painfully aware. *Romeo and Juliet* ends with a double suicide, and—believe it or not—has been the target of censorship efforts as a result.[13] Suicide is an issue in literally countless other plays, novels, operas, songs, and works of visual art. That people, including kids, fantasize about, contemplate, and consume art on these subjects doesn't mean that artworks which recognize and reflect these feelings will cause anyone to act them out. As Jimi Hendrix observed, art and music may have exactly the opposite, cathartic, effect.

Youth music has always been rebellious. Like adolescence itself, it's about new, powerful, and often confusing emotions and experiences. Frustration, aggression, alienation, and of course sexuality, are naturally major topics. Even the term rock 'n' roll was originally a euphemism for sex.

Sexual desire, of course, has been a theme not only in rock, but in blues, country music, jazz, musical comedy, and opera. Violence and sadism are also common themes throughout the arts, and their fascination is not limited to teenage fans of heavy-metal music. It would be hard to beat the French national anthem, the Marseillaise, for sheer bloodcurdling lyrics. In the visual arts, Goya, Dürer, Caravaggio, Bruegel, Rubens, and Rembrandt are a few of the greats who depicted sadistic scenes in often grueling detail—scenes usually taken from life. In 1992, New York's Metropolitan Museum of Art mounted an exhibition honoring the seventeenth-century artist Jusepe de Ribera, whose huge canvases showing scenes of Christian martyrdom are almost unbearably graphic. In one of them, an executioner gleefully sharpens the knife he will use to flay the victim.[14]

The perils and joys of inebriation have also been themes not only in music but in poetry and other literature, from nineteenth-century greats such as Coleridge and Baudelaire to twentieth-century masters of the hallucinatory such as William Burroughs. Burroughs's drug-drenched novel *Naked Lunch* (also, of course, censored in its time) surely rivals any blues or rock creation that describes the highs and lows induced by chemistry.

Drug experimentation is part of human experience, and all human experience is reflected in art. Suppressing all art or information about alcohol or drugs won't help produce kids with sensible attitudes on the subject; in fact, suppressing the subject makes it all the more tempting and intriguing. What's needed is more information, not a conspiracy of silence.

Of all the arts, music has probably from earliest times been humanity's most direct expression of the irrational, "Dionysian" side of life. One critic has said of rock 'n' roll that "in the hands of gentleman rockers like Jackson Browne or Dan Fogelberg" it can be "sweet and tender, even uplifting," but "in the hands of a Prince, an AC-DC, a Midnight Oil, or a group like the Sex Pistols" it can be "savage, brutal, and filled with an erotic ferociousness that scares the holy shit out of adult authority figures and right-wing conservatives." He explains:

> Rock music has a power—most certainly—over its constituents, but the power is not hypnosis. Rock lyrics like those in Prince's "Darling Nikki" do not necessarily lead listeners to masturbate in a hotel lobby with the latest edition of *Esquire*. To those who love it, rock is a celebration of life, an escape from the world's adversity, or a means of stating independence from the powerful bureaucratic forces that rule all of our lives.[15]

The Labeling Campaign Goes Legislative
and the "Parental Advisory" Label Comes of Age

The 1985 Senate hearings and the RIAA's tepid promise to encourage labeling did not make the issue of naughty lyrics go away. The PMRC, joined by fundamentalist pressure groups, continued its well-publicized assaults on sex, drugs, and rock 'n' roll. By 1989, at least sixteen state legislatures were considering bills that would require warning labels on pop music with frowned-upon content, similar in most respects to the PMRC's original list. Some of the bills would also have criminalized the sale of labeled recordings to minors.

In this respect—because the forbidden subjects included not just sex but drugs, violence, occultism, and so on—the proposals went far beyond what the First Amendment allows in the way of restricting minors' access to art or entertainment. Both "obscenity" and "harmful to minors" laws bar the sale of some artistic expression with sexual themes, but talk or art about violence, drugs, suicide, and the occult have full constitutional protection. This may seem a strange inversion of values—to censor depictions of lovemaking but not of violence—but the answer is not to add violence to the list of forbidden subjects. We shouldn't punish or suppress *any* creative expression; rather, we should listen to its messages and then critique them or the underlying attitudes and realities they reflect.

New Jersey's labeling bill was typical of the broad sweep of the music censorship proposals introduced in 1989. This legislation would have required the labeling of any musical recording "containing lyrics which explicitly describe, advocate, or encourage suicide, incest, bestiality, sadomasochism, rape or involuntary sexual penetration, or which advocate or encourage murder, ethnic, racial or religious intimidation, the use of illegal drugs or the excessive or illegal use of alcohol." The label had to specify which of the forbidden topics was present—"morbid violence," "suicide," and so on. Selling an unlabeled album to a teenager if the music "described, advocated, or encouraged" any of these things was a crime. Yet trying to decide what constitutes advocacy or encouragement is no easy task, especially in rock music, where lyrics may be barely audible above the din.

Opponents were quick to point out that under bills like New Jersey's, a long list of treasured songs would have to be labeled and withheld from anyone under eighteen, including "Waltzing Matilda" (suicide), "Goodnight Irene" (suicide), "She'll be Coming 'Round the Mountain" (incest), "Frankie and Johnny" (sexual conduct in a violent context), "Beer Barrel Polka" (alcohol), and most of the world's great operas, from "Tosca" (murder, suicide, and steamy sexual lyrics) to "Tristan und Isolde" (adulterous sex and suicide again).

By 1990, the threat of a bewildering array of different legal requirements in as many as eighteen states that were considering music labeling and censorship bills persuaded the recording industry that a more visible response was called for. Like the movie production companies that established the Hays Code in the thirties, and the film rating system more recently, the recording industry evidently felt that self-censorship in some form was necessary to silence its critics and ward off threats of oppressive governmental action. So in 1990 the RIAA announced that it had designed its own "Parental Advisory/Explicit Lyrics" label, with a distinctive logo, to be made available to music producers.

Most of the major record companies adopted the logo within the year, though each decided independently when to use it. The

RIAA suggested no guidelines for when the label would be appropriate; unlike the movie industry's trade association, the MPAA, which itself controls application of the PG, R, and other film ratings, the RIAA would take no part in deciding which musical releases should be labeled. Nor, according to the RIAA, were the labels to be interpreted as passing judgment on whether the stickered albums were unsuitable for people under a given age.

Despite these fond hopes, however, the "explicit lyrics" label has been interpreted in just this way by those eager to censor the messages of popular music. By the spring of 1991, lyrics-labeling bills were again being considered in eight states, and this time, some of them *incorporated* the RIAA labels as a way of determining when an album couldn't be sold to minors. Louisiana's bill, for example, criminalized the sale to minors of any recording:

> which has as its basic theme the advocation [*sic*] or encourage-
> ment of rape, incest, bestiality, sadomasochism, prostitution,
> homicide, unlawful ritualistic acts, suicide, the commission of a
> crime upon the person or property of another because of his sex,
> race, color, religion, or national origin, the use of any controlled
> dangerous substance . . . or the unlawful use of alcohol *and*
> *which contains thereon* a label or other indicator suggesting that
> its lyrics may be explicit. (Emphasis added.)

Like the New Jersey bill, Louisiana's raised many intriguing questions. What is an "unlawful ritualistic act"? When does a song that mentions beer, wine, or whiskey "encourage" its "unlawful use"? And how are distributors and retailers to figure out whether song lyrics that address or refer to a homicide, for example, or a racially motivated crime, "advocate" or "encourage" the various acts that are mentioned?

In addition, the Louisiana bill relied on the RIAA label to trigger penalties. This additional element was crucial: because it would be so difficult to predict what a prosecutor might decide constituted "advocacy" or "encouragement" in a musical work, the clearly predictable result of Louisiana's proposed law would have been to force music stores to rely on the RIAA label as a shortcut to deciding what albums and artists should be eliminated. This bill passed the legislature two years running and was only stopped with a governor's veto.

The new stream of legislative proposals wasn't the only negative fallout from the adoption of the "explicit lyrics" label. Politicians and pressure groups also began to rely on the labels to identify the albums they wanted to attack. Although the RIAA insisted that its label did not mean music stores should refuse to sell certain recordings to minors, the warning was simply too tempting and convenient a shortcut for censors. It was certainly easier to rely on the industry warning label than actually to listen to all those albums before deciding what was objectionable. Thus, even without legislation to back them up, prosecutors, either on their own initiative or spurred on by procensorship pressure groups, began to ask, urge, or even order stores to segregate labeled recordings and/or refrain from selling them to teenagers (see Chapter 3 for more on how this process works).

In Guilderland, New York, in early 1992, for example, the police chief sent a letter to all local music stores warning them about "illegal selling" of labeled recordings, citing New York's obscenity law. He failed to mention that the labels bore no relation whatever to the legal question of obscenity, and in many instances didn't even indicate that an album's lyrics had to do with sex. One journalist quoted an RIAA official as protesting that the labels certainly were not adopted "as a method for law enforcement officials to prohibit the sale of material to minors," but commented rue-fully: "For now, that has been the effect."[16]

After criticism from the ACLU, which pointed out the legal deficiencies in his reasoning, the Guilderland police chief retracted his letter. But it is hard to know how many similar letters, or more informal warnings, have gone out to music stores since the early 1990s without later retractions.

Some music stores have blacklisted labeled recordings without even a nudge from law enforcement. In 1985, at the height of the PMRC brouhaha, Camelot Music and Video, the nation's second-largest retail chain, announced that its stores would not carry labeled recordings. "We're mall-oriented retailers, and what happens if these groups start picketing our stores, and mall developers tell us we cannot carry certain records?" an executive vice president of the company asked.[17]

Indeed, shopping mall leases typically forbid stores from stocking "adult" material, so the "explicit lyrics" label virtually guar-antees trouble for chain stores that rent space in malls. Other major retailers like Sears and J. C. Penney also announced that they wouldn't carry stickered albums.

Soon after the RIAA announcement of the new uniform label, other music stores decided to avoid labeled music. Disc Jockey, a chain with 199 stores, proclaimed that it wouldn't carry any labeled records; while Trans World, with more than 450 stores, said it would require proof of age. This was despite the absence of *any standard* governing when an album gets labeled—not even the amorphous standards found in some of the pro-posed labeling laws. Nor is there any legal basis for stores unilaterally to refrain from selling labeled recordings to minors or anybody else.

One commentator summed up the situation:

Labels offer parental guidance, sure. But how many kids shop for records with their parents? As the PMRC must realize, labeling is useful in one way only. Many, perhaps most, stores and malls will ban X-rated music, creating enormous economic pressure on artists and studios to produce non-X music. That's how the movie ratings work. It amounts to an elegant form of censorship—elegant because it is censorship made to look like consumer information. Who's against consumer information?[18]

Trouble in Omaha

In early 1992, four music stores in Omaha, Nebraska, were charged with violating the state's "harmful to minors" law because they allegedly sold 2 Live Crew's latest recording, *Sports Weekend*, to teenagers. The teenagers had been sent into the stores by their parents and other adults, members of a group called Omaha for Decency. Two of the stores were owned by Trans World, the national chain, and two were owned by a Nebraska company called Pickles. Both companies had already established policies against selling some, but not all, labeled recordings—including those by 2 Live Crew—to minors.

Nebraska's "harmful to minors" law followed the *Miller* v. *California* formula, as modified for youthful consumers (see Chapter 1). Forbidden were materials that appealed to minors' prurient interest; lacked serious literary, artistic, political, or scientific value for minors; and were patently offensive, by adult standards, regarding what's suitable for minors. As with all obscenity laws, the vagueness and subjectivity of Nebraska's definitions were mind-boggling. They meant that music store owners, in common with retailers of books, magazines, and films, could never be quite sure what they could or couldn't sell, if the material referred to sex at all. This was especially true since minors, who range from one day to seventeen years of age, have wildly different tastes, interests, levels of understanding, stages of sexual development, and capacities for artistic appreciation.

The ACLU, representing Pickles, geared up for defending against the charges by consulting with political science professor and rap music expert Carlton Long. But just two weeks before the trials were to start, the Omaha prosecutor, Gary Bucchino, agreed to drop the charges. A federal appeals court decision reversing the 1990 Florida ruling that 2 Live Crew's *As Nasty as They Wanna Be* was legally obscene had just recently come down, and it suggested that a prosecutor attempting to prove the obscenity of popular music would have to do more than simply play the record for a presumably shocked jury and wait for the desired judgment of condemnation. The state would now have to mount more of a case—most likely including expert witnesses who presumably would attest to the work's *lack* of serious value—before it could suppress a piece of music.

In exchange for dismissing the charges, prosecutor Bucchino wanted Trans World and Pickles to make a statement agreeing not to sell *Sports Weekend* to minors, and to abide by the "harmful to minors" law in the future. This sounded acceptable at first blush, considering that the stores already had these policies, but formulating the actual terms of the settlement was trickier.

Bucchino, undoubtedly beset by the usual puzzlement about how to define "harmful to minors," started out by demanding that the stores state they would not sell anything "sexually explicit" to those under eighteen. He either failed to appreciate or chose to ignore that even for young people not all explicit discussion of sex is "patently offensive," appeals to "prurient interest," and lacks value. The final agreement in Omaha dispensed with any attempt to define what "harmful to minors" meant except by reference to the law itself. But the agreement also acknowledged that "more stringent methods" were needed to prevent future sales of "this material" to minors. And it left the stores with little assurance that they wouldn't be prosecuted again for sale of some other album that Bucchino or Omaha for Decency decided was not to their liking.

As Luther Campbell of 2 Live Crew often remarked, it was a mystery how law enforcement officers found so much time to spend listening to and transcribing song lyrics when real crimes such as robbery, rape, drug dealing, and murder continue to go unchecked on the streets of our cities.

❧ 5 ❧

Getting Naked: Censorship of Nudity in Art, Theater, and Dance

Since the human body is the most perfect of all forms, we cannot see it too often.

—Kenneth Clark, *The Nude*[1]

There's a difference between nude and naked.

—Anne-Imelda Radice[2]

Naked in Chattanooga

ENNETH TYNAN WAS AN ICONOCLASTIC BRITISH INTEL-lectual and theater critic who decided in the mid-sixties that it was about time to upgrade the classic striptease for a more sophisticated audience, and in the process to take a satiric look at the interesting sexual habits of *Homo sapiens*. Tynan asked the American theater director and lyricist Jacques Levy to help him with the idea and put together a high-quality musical revue that would incorporate nudity and test the current limits of sexual freedom in theater art.

In Levy's hands, Tynan's idea began to evolve. Levy recruited an impressive array of international talent to write parts of the script, among them the Irish literary icon Samuel Beckett, the rock 'n' roll poet John Lennon, the satirist and cartoonist Jules Feiffer, and the then up-and-coming playwright Sam Shepard.

The finished work was a hybrid, combining dance sequences with skits and jokes satirizing everything from generational differences in sexual frankness to Masters and Johnson–style sex research to differing tastes in pornography. Among the highlights were a coy but restrained opening number that lampooned the traditional prurient striptease, some sophomoric sexual humor, a gorgeous nude *pas de deux* accompanied by a folk music ballad, and other occasional glimpses of well-muscled bare flesh. They called the work *Oh! Calcutta!*—a play on the bawdy French exclamation, *Oh, quel cul tu as!* (Oh, what an ass you have!) With its episodic structure, innovative lighting and design, sequences of nudity, and frankness about sex, the play was a stylistic groundbreaker for American theater.

It opened in New York in 1969, off-Broadway, was a smash success, reopened on Broadway in the mid-seventies and became, for a time, Broadway's longest-running musical. In the late seventies and eighties the show toured nationally and internationally. In the early nineties, it was still touring.

In 1991 the *Oh! Calcutta!* roadshow inquired about booking one of the two municipal theaters in Chattanooga, Tennessee. These are the only two venues in Chattanooga appropriate for staging a big musical. The city said no: *Oh! Calcutta!* could not be staged there. Municipal officials claimed that the show violated city and state "public indecency" laws, and besides, it was legally obscene.

Laws against public nudity or "indecency" are intended to protect citizens from the presumed shock, offense, and embarrassment of being subjected to exhibitionist behavior in parks, subways, or other public places. Chattanooga's idea was to apply these general laws to theater: after all, theaters are open to the public, so it could be argued that the shows performed there take place in "public places." The city thus wanted to use laws intended to protect unwitting individuals from exposure to nudity and apply them to consenting audiences who generally knew what they were getting and didn't mind—indeed, may have come to the show for that very purpose.

The Supreme Court Holds Forth

The Chattanooga city fathers took courage in their quest from a recent decision of the U.S. Supreme Court. *Barnes* v. *Glen Theatre*, decided in June 1991, approved the State of Indiana's use of its general law against "public nudity" to ban nude barroom dancing. The *Barnes* decision came as a surprise to the worlds of both art and constitutional law much more because of its reasoning than its result. For in upholding the State of Indiana's requirement that dancers at the city of South Bend's Kitty Kat Lounge wear the minimal coverings of a G-string and pasties, several members of the Supreme Court seemed to use reasoning that could apply equally well to nudity in theater, opera, and ballet.

Chief Justice William Rehnquist wrote an opinion announcing the judgment of the Court in *Barnes*, though only two other justices (Sandra Day O'Connor and Anthony Kennedy) agreed with his reasoning. Rehnquist started by acknowledging, reluctantly, that nude dancing was a form of artistic expression, whose primary message was "eroticism and sexuality." Nonetheless, he noted, laws against public nudity were part of our history, traceable to "the Bible story of Adam and Eve." The state's minimal requirement of pasties and G-string was justified by its interest in "protecting order and morality," and would "not deprive the dance of whatever erotic message it conveys; it simply makes the message slightly less graphic."[3]

Chief Justice Rehnquist did not explain why he thought this was so. The dancers and their audience certainly might disagree. In

fact, artists who use nudity, from barroom dancers to opera directors, probably do so with a specific set of messages in mind. Pasties,
G-strings, and the like, may very well interfere.

Oh! Calcutta! provides a good example. As Jacques Levy testified in the Chattanooga case, the idea of *Oh! Calcutta!* was to present human nudity as a symbol of grace, purity, openness, and
freedom. Tawdry adornments commonly associated with barroom
entertainment are likely to destroy the effect.

Justice David Souter seemed to recognize the problematic
implications of Rehnquist's reasoning in *Barnes*. He wrote a separate opinion, agreeing with the result but arguing that nudity in
entertainment could not be banned simply because of some vague
public interest in "morality." According to Souter, it was the "secondary effects" of clubs like the Kitty Kat Lounge that justified
Indiana's rule. In his words, "prostitution, sexual assault, and associated crimes" are well known to be found in the same parts of town
as nude barroom dancing.

Justice Souter didn't explain how Indiana's pasties and G-string
requirement would solve the problem of "harmful secondary
effects." Certainly, it didn't seem likely that these minor additions
to the dancers' anatomy would have an appreciable impact on prostitution, sexual assault, or anything else that might occur in the
vicinity of erotic dancing establishments. Nor, for that matter, was
there any basis for assuming that nude dancing *caused* sexual assault
or prostitution, or that such problems would be reduced in an area
if nude dancing were eliminated.

Justice Souter's rationale for supporting the result in *Barnes*
was elitist, as the dissenting justices angrily pointed out. It would
deprive Joe Six-pack of the entertainment that classical dance and
opera-goers could enjoy. But at least Souter's opinion held out the
hope that dance and theater not purveyed in the red-light districts

of town would escape censorship by government antinudity inspectors.

Justice Antonin Scalia, on the other hand, didn't make such distinctions. Scalia thought the nude dancing case didn't raise any First Amendment concerns because Indiana was simply applying a neutral law against public indecency. That is, there was no evidence that the Indiana legislature that passed the law *intended* to interfere with artistic freedom. And to Scalia, intent was all that mattered: it was irrelevant that the law's *effect* was to censor art.

Scalia's logic would presumably permit a state to prosecute theaters that produced not only *Oh! Calcutta!* but also plays like *Equus, M. Butterfly, Frankie and Johnny in the Clair de Lune,* or *Marat/Sade.* This last work, produced in America in 1969 by England's Royal Shakespeare Company, included a nude Marat emerging from his bathtub, "crystallizing for the audience just how unprotected and vulnerable" the French revolutionary leader had become by the end of his life.[4]

In his separate opinion in *Barnes,* Justice Souter took issue specifically with Justice Scalia's implication that nudity in theater could be banned. Souter said that it was "difficult to see how the enforcement of Indiana's statute against nudity in a production of 'Hair' or 'Equus' somewhere other than an 'adult' theater would further the State's interest in avoiding harmful secondary effects."

Using Barnes in Chattanooga

When they denied citizens of Chattanooga the right to see *Oh! Calcutta!* in 1991, the city officials evidently wanted to test the limits of the Supreme Court's ruling in *Barnes.* They also wanted to vindicate their city after its defeat sixteen years before in another Supreme Court case involving nudity. That earlier decision, *Southeastern Promotions* v. *Conrad,* had concerned the classic 1960s

"American tribal love-rock musical," *Hair*. In one brief scene, the cast members of *Hair* strip to their birthday suits in celebration of the Age of Aquarius, but, as a critic commented at the time, "with all that uproar going on behind, it's probably the unsexiest nude scene ever to have been devised."[5]

Hair encountered censorship problems when it began to tour the country in the early seventies. Sometimes local authorities protested that the show was obscene, sometimes that it violated public nudity laws, sometimes simply that their municipal theater was just like a private one—not open to all comers—and therefore had a right to decide what it wanted to present. In Chattanooga in 1971 as in 1991, the only theaters capable of housing a substantial musical production were municipally owned, and the city simply said no to *Hair*.

Southeastern Promotions, the producer of the show, sued Chattanooga. The company claimed that the municipal theater was like a street or park: owned by the government but open to the public for all manner of free speech doings—a public forum where the government couldn't pick and choose who spoke, sang, acted, or danced there, any more than it could decide which political parties or viewpoints got a permit to hold a rally at the local park.

The Supreme Court agreed. In a major First Amendment decision, the Court ruled that Chattanooga's municipal theaters were public forums, and the city couldn't unilaterally deny access to them. If Chattanooga thought the proposed show unlawful, it had to go to court promptly to get a full, impartial adjudication of the issue.

When Singer Entertainment sought to book *Oh! Calcutta!* in Chattanooga twenty years later, the city sent a delegation up to Nashville, where the show was then on view, to see for themselves. The delegation reported that *Oh! Calcutta!* was really too much for their fellow citizens to handle. Chattanooga's attorneys then followed the procedural requirements laid down in the case involving *Hair* and sued Singer Entertainment. They asked for a court judgment that the show could be banned because it violated both the public nudity and obscenity laws.

Chattanooga's obscenity argument was a bit of a surprise. Under the three-part *Miller* v. *California* obscenity test, a work had to lack serious value, appeal to a prurient—that is, a "shameful or morbid"—interest in sex, and depict sex in a "patently offensive" way before it could be found obscene. Yet it seemed unlikely that *Oh! Calcutta!* could be thought patently offensive by current standards in 1991. It had been a long-running hit on Broadway; it had been presented on tour all over the world and in many American cities; and it was extremely *non*graphic compared to the books, magazines, videos, R-rated films, and cable TV readily available in most parts of the country, including Chattanooga, in 1991. Its sexual jokes and skits were dated (some were arguably in bad taste), but it could hardly be said that they appealed to a shameful or morbid interest in sex. Finally, *Oh! Calcutta!*'s dance sequences had obvious artistic value. The show had political value in its satires of, for example, Masters and Johnson–type sex research, or married couples trying to revive their failing sex lives. Its scripts had literary value; at least, one might presume this of works by the likes of Samuel Beckett, John Lennon, Sam Shepard, and Jules Feiffer.

But the city argued that times had changed since the unbuttoned sixties. Standards were less liberal now, at least in Chattanooga. At trial, the city's lawyer even argued that *Oh! Calcutta!* promoted sexual promiscuity, which "caused" AIDS; ergo, the show should be banned.

The judge in the case, R. Vann Owens, decided to empanel an "advisory jury." Since this was a civil suit and it sought only a court order, not money damages, no jury was necessary. But the judge

evidently wanted to take the community's pulse on the subjective—
and touchy—obscenity issue.

The jurors, after hearing four days of evidence, including testimony by Jacques Levy and other experts, and watching a video of
Oh! Calcutta!, advised Judge Vann Owens that although they
thought the show was patently offensive, they didn't think it was
obscene: it had serious value and lacked appeal to prurient interest.
The judge reluctantly agreed with their conclusion, but could not
resist emphasizing his distaste for the production. "Presumably," he
wrote in an opinion shortly after the trial, "the play's overall theme
is one of advocating a more casual or relaxed attitude toward sex" (a
bit of an oversimplification, but more or less accurate). He went on:

> If the play was intended to advocate freer sex, it was more appro-
> priate in the late 1960s when it was written. The horror of the
> AIDS epidemic which has resulted from casual sex makes any
> such advocacy especially untimely today. In any event, however, it
> is not the popular, intelligent or sensible messages that need the
> protection of the First Amendment. The guarantee of free speech
> is *most* important in its role as protector of unpopular and seem-
> ingly unworthy messages. Whatever little value the play might
> have, the First Amendment normally protects against prior
> restraint where the production is not obscene under the legal test.

To say that Judge Vann Owens missed the point here would be
to put it mildly. Sensuality and openness, not promiscuity, is the
point of *Oh! Calcutta!* As critic Jack Kroll wrote in 1969,

> those who react in anger to the making public of the most inti-
> mate of human concerns are missing the point. In a sense all art
> is about failure and possibility and *Oh! Calcutta!* is evoking the
> failures and possibilities of our most basic equipment and
> behavior.[6]

Judge Vann Owens did not ask the jury for advice on *Oh! Calcutta!*'s alleged violation of Tennessee's public nudity law. In his posttrial opinion, the judge avoided this issue by saying that the predicted illegal conduct hadn't yet occurred. There would be time enough to arrest somebody for public nudity if and when it did.

The city never appealed the judge's ruling, so any hopes Chattanooga might have had of retrying the *Hair* case of twenty years before slipped by. *Oh! Calcutta!* played without incident, though with less than a full house, in part because of convoluted ticket sales requirements imposed by the city and strongly encouraged by the judge—to ensure that no minors would get into the theater. There were no "public nudity" arrests.

"The Naked Human Body Was the Central Subject of Art"

Oh! Calcutta! was a stylistic groundbreaker for its use of nudity in serious theater, but Kenneth Tynan and Jacques Levy were hardly alone. By the late sixties and early seventies, nudity had become increasingly common on the European and American stage.

In the Royal Shakespeare Company's 1968 production of Christopher Marlowe's *Dr. Faustus*, for example, the hero's vision of Helen of Troy was embodied in actress Maggie Wright's nude procession, "silent and naked across the stage." Given that Faust's interest in the mythical Helen was sexual, this was "exactly the beautiful vision that Faustus might have had."[7] Similarly, in one staging of Richard Wagner's *Tannhäuser*, the opening scene orgy featured dancers nude except for G-strings, as they simulated a variety of sexual positions; Venus, played by the English soprano Gwyneth Jones, was bare-breasted for most of the show. All this steamy sexuality certainly dramatized the hero's more-than-three-hour struggle to resist the temptations of physical love.

If nudity is still a relatively new development in live theater and opera, it's as old as civilization itself in the visual arts. The earliest Greek sculptures, called *kouroi*, were male nudes, and fascination with beautiful, well-proportioned young males persisted through the golden age of ancient Greek culture. Roman artists copied the Greeks, turning out thousands of statues celebrating the beauty, grace, harmony, proportion, and sensuality—but sometimes also the struggle and suffering—that can be expressed by the nude human form.

Christianity changed the nude in visual art and made it an image of shame. Consistent with the Church's view of sexual knowledge as the primal sin, medieval nudes often appeared slouched and guilt-ridden. As scholar Kenneth Clark has written:

> The body inevitably changed its status. It ceased to be the mirror
> of divine perfection and became an object of humiliation and
> shame. . . . While the Greek nude began with the heroic body
> proudly displaying itself in the palaestra, the Christian nude
> began with the muddled body cowering in consciousness of sin.[8]

The Catholic Church strived mightily to control nudity in both painting and sculpture throughout the Middle Ages and well into the Renaissance. Under Church decrees, nudity was permitted for classical mythological themes but not for religious ones.

By the Renaissance, though, Church censorship was becoming a lost cause, as artists began to revive the classical tradition. Michelangelo's *David* is only the most famous of his gorgeous well-muscled male nudes. Donatello's *David* is even more frankly homo-erotic in its pose. Caravaggio's males also have a definite come-hither look.

Nor were the glories of the female anatomy ignored. Botticelli's *Birth of Venus* is one of the more celebrated examples. Another of the innumerable Renaissance Venuses, by Lorenzo Lotto, has Cupid urinating onto the goddess's naked torso. The notes to this work, which hangs in New York's Metropolitan Museum of Art, explain that it is a marriage painting, and the urine is "an augury of fertility."

The sinewy figures that Michelangelo painted struggling in the throes of *The Last Judgment* on the walls of the Sistine Chapel in Rome were also originally nudes. Pope Paul IV had their private parts painted over with drapery in 1558. Indeed, *The Last Judgment*, despite its brilliance and its religious content, barely survived at all. Another pope seriously considered having the masterpiece destroyed.

As the Catholic Church's political hegemony weakened, the naked human form regained its rightful place in Western art, but the ideological struggle continued. From Francisco de Goya's luxuriant *Nude Maja* in 1796 to the palpably sensual women painted by Gustave Courbet, Jean-Auguste Ingres, and others in nineteenth-century France, nudes frequently evoked outraged responses.

The now-common sense of the word "nude" came into use, in fact, as a defense of artists' fascination with the human form against the continuing attacks of church and state. The word was "forced into our vocabulary by critics of the early eighteenth century to persuade the artless islanders that, in countries where painting and sculpture were practiced and valued as they should be, the naked human body was the central subject of art."[9]

The semantic distinction, however, didn't always help. In 1769 the Royal Academy of London prohibited any art student under age twenty, unless married, from drawing female nudes from live models. Fifteen years later a nude Venus elicited such outrage in Philadelphia that it was removed from public view. Philadelphia saw some progress in 1806 when the Pennsylvania Academy of Fine Arts presented an exhibit of ancient nude statues and set aside one day for "ladies." Even so, "indecent" statues had to be draped. A nude painting displayed in New York in 1815 was denounced as "a deplorable example of European depravity."[10]

Much depended on how a nude was presented. In the nineteenth century, two female nudes by Edouard Manet caused major scandals, not so much because they were unclothed as because of their unashamed, casual, and decidedly contemporary air. *Dejeuner sur l'herbe* shows a naked woman unselfconsciously poised on the grass in a country setting, picnicking with two fully dressed young men. One outraged critic called her "a commonplace woman of the demi-monde, as naked as can be, shamelessly lolling between two dandies."[11] Manet's *Olympia*, obviously a courtesan, provoked a similar reaction.

Fear and loathing of the human nude reached new heights during the Victorian Era in both England and the United States. The new prudery coincided, of course, with enactment of the first obscenity laws in both nations. Under the prevailing obscenity standards, the U.S. government considered any pictorial nudity to violate the law—a view that lasted well into the twentieth century.

Accordingly, in 1933, the U.S. Customs Bureau seized books containing reproductions of Michelangelo's *Last Judgment* fresco in its original nude state. The government notified the art gallery that had ordered the books that it had "detained . . . a package addressed to you containing obscene photo books, 'Ceiling Sistine Chapel,' Filles Michel Angelo, the importation of which is held to be prohibited under the provisions of the Tariff Act."[12] An attorney in the Customs Bureau later ordered that the books be released.

Theatrical Nudity and the Culture War

Nudity cannot be equated with obscenity. It may be brief and fleeting; it may consist only of a baby's buttocks; it may be informational rather than erotic. As one observer noted years ago, it certainly might be presumed that "a young woman of today would possess sufficient anatomical knowledge not to be shocked by the sight of an unclothed fellow creature of her own species."[13]

Yet fear of the unclothed human form remains a mysterious aspect of some societies, including the United States. Today, censorship of theater nudity goes well beyond the occasional fiat by a local government like Chattanooga's. It informs every phase of our culture wars, from government funding decisions to art exhibitions to school curriculums and paintings hanging on classroom walls.

In Charlotte, North Carolina, in 1990, police instructed the Spirit Square Theater that its production of *Frankie and Johnny in the Clair de Lune*, by the American playwright Terrence McNally, could not continue unless a brief glimpse of nudity in the first act was excised. The police said it violated indecent exposure laws. The show's director quickly acquiesced: "Spirit Square is a big organization," he said, "but nobody can afford this kind of legal case."[14]

Frankie and Johnny takes place entirely in Frankie's apartment, where she and Johnny have just made love. The movie version with Michelle Pfeiffer and Al Pacino changed the sets but kept much of the theme—the struggle for romantic commitment in uncertain times. Given that the play is about sexual love, and involves a lot of getting in and out of bed, the brief nudity didn't seem out of order. As the *Charlotte Observer* editorialized, the police mandate was "a flagrant example of using the law to enforce prudish nonsense. . . . Spirit Square is hardly Billy Bob's Beer Joint and Bottomless Emporium, after all, and a law that makes no distinction between the two is a nutty law indeed."

Sometimes, theatrical nudity has been censored without the government's getting involved. Boise, Idaho's Shakespeare Festival in 1991 was to present Frank Wedekind's *Spring Awakening*, a nine-teenth-century work about adolescent sexuality and rebellion. When the board of the Boise festival discovered what was afoot, they ordered the director to excise the nudity. He resigned instead. Idahoans never got to see *Spring Awakening*.

Performance artist Karen Finley, who was denied a National Endowment for the Arts grant in 1990 because of the controversial nature of her shows, uses nudity for dramatic, rather than porno-graphic purposes. (See Chapter 6 for more on the arts funding con-troversy and the Finley case.) Finley's nudity as she rages against sexism, homophobia, homelessness, AIDS, and violence against women emphasizes, if anything, the vulnerability, not the allure, of the unclothed female body. But as a result of Finley's radical style, she's widely known simply as the "nude, chocolate-smeared woman."

Not all theaters have caved in to prudery, though. In 1990 the New York City Opera was preparing to present *Moses und Aron*, by the twentieth-century composer Arnold Schoenberg. The opera tells the familiar story of the two biblical characters, the Hebrews' wanderings through the wilderness, and their worship of the Golden Calf. The script at one point calls for "four naked virgins" and a full-scale orgy.

Given then-recent controversies at the NEA, and the New York City Opera's reliance on NEA grants and the private matching funds they are so good at generating, some people began to question whether the virgins in *Moses und Aron* really had to be naked. As one critic reported, "in the nervousness over offending the religious con-servatives who have mounted an attack on the . . . Endowment, City Opera officials worried about the impact of those four virgins."[15] But the result in New York was happier than in Charlotte, North Carolina, or Boise, Idaho: the City Opera overcame its quivers and decided to stick with Schoenberg. Artistic integrity, and nakedness, prevailed.

The same season, the Kennedy Center in Washington, D.C., presented a production of Richard Strauss's opera, *Salome*, also based on a lurid biblical tale. In the story, King Herod is so besotted with Salome's beauty and sensuality that he offers her anything if she will dance for him. It turns out she wants the head of John the Baptist, which, once delivered, she proceeds to kiss and fondle in a manner that would probably meet any censorship board's definition of sexual perversity.

Salome's famous "Dance of the Seven Veils" is often a staging problem for buxom sopranos, but it wasn't for the Washington Opera's star, Maria Ewing. According to published reports, her performance of the famous striptease was utterly persuasive. At the end, she "stood downstage, naked in bright moonlight, for what seemed a long interrupted climax. It was easy to understand why Herod had promised her anything."[16]

Like the New York City Opera, the Washington Opera wasn't unaware of the risks that a nude Salome created for the company's funding prospects. Ever since 1913, when New York's Metropolitan Opera was pressured into withdrawing a planned production of *Salome*, the work has provoked scandal. Oscar Wilde's play, on which the opera is based, was banned in London when it was first produced. There was considerable speculation in 1990 that *Salome* "might encounter similar trouble from the Helmsmen"—Senator Jesse Helms—and other "Cultural Commissars."[17]

However, the show went forward without incident—to wild acclaim, in fact. Perhaps Senator Helms and others who had attacked the NEA for funding work no different in spirit but less culturally sacrosanct saw *Salome* as a losing battle.

This did not, however, prevent Helms in 1991 from complaining on the floor of the U.S. Senate about a New York Shakespeare Festival production of *A Midsummer Night's Dream* in which the fairies were all nude or nearly so. Helms failed to note that no federal money had been received for the show. The Shakespeare Festival's longtime director, Joseph Papp, had refused NEA funding after the agency created a requirement in 1989 that recipients would have to sign an oath agreeing not to produce any artwork that might be deemed obscene. (See Chapter 6 for more on this "obscenity oath.")

Naked Kids

A word should be said about child nudes. In the 1980s, partly in response to genuine concern over the sexual abuse of children, but partly also because of rising censorship pressures against nudity and sexuality in art, child pornography laws were amended and expanded. To the extent these laws punish the sexual abuse of children, no responsible citizen could reasonably quarrel with their purpose. But to the extent they punish nude photography of children and teenagers, they've turned out to be a major censorship problem.

That problem came most dramatically to light in April 1990 when a respected San Francisco art photographer, Jock Sturges, opened his apartment door to find federal and state police poised to embark on a massive search and seizure of all his photographic prints, negatives, and equipment, as well as his business records. It took Sturges and his attorneys a year and a half to get his property returned (most of his photos were not even nudes). During this time, the FBI conducted an extensive investigation, which carried even to Germany and France as well as throughout the U.S., seeking evidence that Sturges and those who purchased his work

were pedophiles and child pornographers. FBI agents demanded
that art galleries representing Sturges turn over their customer lists.
The government never found any evidence of crime, and a federal
grand jury ultimately refused to indict Sturges based on his nude
photography.

This near-two-year nightmare started for Sturges because he
photographed child nudes, sometimes singly, sometimes in family
groups. Many of the photos were taken in naturist colonies or nude
beaches in Europe. The kids weren't abused, exploited, or even
uncomfortable; Sturges had releases from their parents; and the
photos were beautiful and nonpornographic—except perhaps to
law enforcement officers who have chosen to spend their careers
investigating and prosecuting in this area. The FBI agents and U.S.
prosecutors who went after Sturges saw sexual exploitation and
lewdness in shots of kids revealing wholesome relaxed comfort with
their bodies.

The laws of the United States and many states contribute
mightily to the problem by defining child pornography to include
"lascivious exhibition of the genitals." What this means is hard to
discern. Surely not all child nudes equal child pornography; but
nudity naturally includes genitalia. Because the U.S. government
sometimes seems to view any photography of children that shows
their genitals to be "lascivious," Jock Sturges is not the only one
who has suffered.

The 1990 obscenity trial of Cincinnati museum director
Dennis Barrie, for example, included two counts of child pornography. Barrie was prosecuted for exhibiting a traveling retrospective
of photographs by the late Robert Mapplethorpe. Two of the
photos in the Mapplethorpe show were of children. One, a
daughter of the artist's friend, was pictured sitting on a bench in a
natural childlike pose, legs apart, her dress carelessly askew so that

part of her vulva is exposed. The child had no look of fear or dis-comfort; the pose was not pornographic but "guileless and charming."[18] The second child photo, *Jessie McBride*, simply showed a little boy nude perched on the back of a chair. Barrie was acquitted by a Cincinnati jury.[19] (See Chapters 1 and 6 for more on the Mapplethorpe controversy.)

Yet the near hysteria over nude children, and grown-ups, con-tinues. Despite the occasional triumph of a naked soprano, despite the occasional acquittal in a criminal case, censorship of simple nudity has become pervasive not only in live theater but in painting, sculpture, and photography. The roots of the hysteria lie deep in American culture, and can produce full-scale "sex panics," particularly in times of economic insecurity or rapid social change.[20] The rise of the religious right in the U.S. has contributed immeasurably to repressive attitudes that, equating nudity with sex-uality and sexuality with shame, ignore the beauty and expressive-ness of the human body.

Examples of the censorship of nude images in the visual arts are abundant. In 1992 an artist who was invited to show her works at the Manhasset Public Library on Long Island was disinvited after the library discovered that nudes were included. In 1991, a community college in upstate New York invited a recent graduate, Maria Monk, to mount a show of her photographs of nudes; after protest from a member of a local religious order, the works were taken down. Only a lawsuit (cosponsored by the ACLU and New York Volunteer Lawyers for the Arts) succeeded in restoring the exhibition.

The year before, a state college in Maryland changed its mind about a show incorporating nonpornographic female nude portraits of the artist and her pregnant friend. No lawsuit was brought although the artist protested (unsuccessfully) through the college's administrative system. In the spring of 1991 a Florida community college removed a copy of a classic Renoir nude, *La Toilette*, from an exhibit touring the college's five campuses. The sixty-one-year-old grandmother who had painted the copy remarked, "It's a shame to make people think there's something wrong with the human body. Art is art." In 1992, at the request of some schools, parents, and religious groups, the Virginia Museum of Fine Arts created a special tour that avoids all the nude works of art. One museum employee acknowledged that the task was difficult. The tours might not stop at any nudes, she noted, "but they certainly will pass by some."[21]

In another Florida incident, in 1991, an award-winning nude by the local college's art instructor was removed; it showed a young woman standing amid lilacs after finishing a swim.[22] The same year, a public high school principal in New Britain, Connecticut, banned three innocent, nonpornographic nudes from a student art show. It was apparently irrelevant that nudes are the first subjects studied in almost any elementary studio art class.

The commercial entertainment industry has not been immune to the wave of bodyphobia. In 1991 Victory Records, under pressure from retail chains, vetoed the cover art for an album by the rock band Tin Machine because it featured reproductions of *kouroi*, the early Greek male nudes. The album as originally designed was marketed in Europe, but in the U.S. the *kouroi* had to have their private parts covered. Before engaging in this bit of self-censorship, the record company had tried to place the original cover art on a Los Angeles billboard, but the Gannett billboard company refused: "We had Rodin's 'Thinker' on bus stops, and we received lots of complaints from citizens and local elected officials," a Gannett officer explained.[23]

Two of the most vivid, and perhaps saddest, instances of censoring nudity in visual art occurred at public educational institutions.

In late 1991 a female professor at Pennsylvania State University's Schuylkill campus complained that the display on a classroom wall of a reproduction of Francisco de Goya's classic *Nude Maja* constituted sexual harassment. She said she found it difficult to appear professional with the sensuous nude hanging on the wall, and that it distracted male students from the lesson at hand. She was supported by the university's Commission for Women, and the reproduction was taken down.

In fact, all four of the art posters in the classroom were removed. Students protested the censorship, but the university responded that this was simply a question of "classroom climate." After a few days, the artworks were rehung in the student lounge.[24]

Penn State's action was not the first trouble for Goya's *Nude Maja* in the United States. In 1959, the U.S. Post Office had banned the mailing of a color reproduction of the work that was being used to promote a movie about Goya's life. (Earlier, the postmaster of the Philippines had held up all issues of *Time* magazine because of a reproduction of the painting in the art section.[25])

Calling the painting sexual harassment today doesn't really change things—it merely justifies censorship with some new rhetoric that on the surface may sound helpful to women but really ends up hurting the cause of female liberation. (See Chapter 7 for more on the dangers to women of censoring art and information about sex.) And it imposes one interpretation on a complex work of art whose message could as easily be viewed not as degrading to women but as a celebration of female independence and sexuality. Perhaps a better remedy for immature male snickering at a classic nude would have been to discuss the issure rather than remove the art.

The other assault on nudity in art happened in Eugene, Oregon, in 1991, when a photograph of Michelangelo's *David*, perhaps the most celebrated work of sculpture in Western history, was censored out of a junior high school TV news report. "Frontal nudity" was the problem, according to a media specialist at the school. "We wouldn't want to show anything parents would be offended by."[26]

❡ **6** ❡

"The Taxpayers' Money": The Question of Government Funding

It is through art that we can understand ourselves.

—National Endowment for the Arts,
Statement of Mission

The NEA

N 1965, WHEN CONGRESS CREATED THE NATIONAL Endowment for the Arts, the idea was to advance artistic freedom and creativity, not government-approved, officially "acceptable" art. To make its desires perfectly clear, Congress wrote into the NEA law, "It is necessary and appropriate for the Federal Government to help create and sustain not only a climate encouraging freedom of thought, imagination, and inquiry, but also the material conditions facilitating this release of creative talent."[1]

Congress recognized the risks to "freedom of thought, imagination, and inquiry" in a federal arts funding program. It didn't take a prophet to foresee the danger of political interference. America, unlike Europe, doesn't have a long tradition of public assistance for the arts. And the best art is often controversial, even confrontational—radical in style as well as substance. It's *supposed* to question the status quo, to shake us out of our complacency, to elicit strong reactions. As one filmmaker has written, the value of artists "is in being obstreperous, outlandish and obscene. Their business is to ignite a revolution of insight in the soul."[2]

New trends in art are almost always ridiculed or condemned. In painting, the Impressionists, the Cubists, the Abstract Expressionists, the Pop artists, were mocked and rejected—and all are now venerated in the most respectable museums. Similarly, the stylistic innovations and frank sexual subject matter of twentieth-century literature were initially greeted with outrage. James Joyce's *Ulysses*, now recognized as a classic, was condemned by one critic at the time of its publication as

> the most infamously obscene book in ancient or modern literature. The obscenity of Rabelais is innocent compared with its leprous and scabrous horrors. All the secret sewers of vice are canalized in its flood of unimaginable thoughts, images and pornographic words. And its unclean lunacies are larded with appalling and revolting blasphemies directed against the Christian religion and against the holy name of Christ—blasphemies hitherto associated with the most degraded orgies and Satanism and the Black Mass.[3]

Ulysses, according to this prominent critic, was not only obscene but blasphemous—certainly no candidate for government funding.

The creators of the National Endowment for the Arts knew this history. The 1965 Senate report on the bill establishing the agency specified that "the fullest attention" must be given "to freedom of artistic and humanistic expression," and added: "Countless times in history artists and humanists who were vilified by their contemporaries because of their innovations in style or mode of expression have become prophets to a later age."

Congress's dilemma was to create an agency insulated enough from political pressures to be able to support innovative, radical, even confrontational work, in addition to funding the already established art presented by museums, concert halls, and repertory theater companies.

This isn't to say that established art is necessarily noncontroversial. Classics from Jean Genet's play *The Maids* to Goya's painting *Nude Maja*, to literary works like Chaucer's *The Miller's Tale* and Aristophanes' *Lysistrata* have been censored by school boards, universities, and private groups in the eighties and nineties. But as a political matter, contemporary art movements that are not yet well-established run the greatest risk of censorship. Centuries or even mere decades of critical approval give a sort of immunity to "pornographic" and "blasphemous" artworks of earlier eras.

Congress needed to find a way to prevent the kind of interference and demagoguery that could easily destroy the integrity of public arts funding. It needed to prevent situations in which pressure groups intent on exploiting hot-button issues—for example, sex, cultural elitism, subversion of traditional values, or perceived insults to organized religion—could publicize, distort, and oversimplify particular works and earn political capital by complaining that these artists or grants offended the American public's moral, political, or religious beliefs.

The result was that the NEA was created with an elaborate "peer panel" structure to insulate Endowment decision-making from partisan pressures. The peer panels, committees of experts in the field, were to review grant applications and make recommendations to the presidentially appointed National Council and chair of the endowment. These political appointees, more vulnerable to instructions from the White House or other outside pressures, would rely on the recommendations of the experts.

That system worked pretty well—for the first twenty-four years. There were, of course, occasional questions raised about particular works during this relatively halcyon time. In 1972, for example, Erica Jong's raunchy best-selling novel, *Fear of Flying*, acknowledged in its flyleaf that an NEA grant had made the writing possible. *Fear of Flying* was shocking to some because it told of sexual adventure from a liberated woman's viewpoint. One congressman complained that taxpayer money was "now supporting the scurrilous and the pornographic, and further, that since ladies were present, a reading of the text would be inappropriate."[4] The irony of this remark, given that a "lady" had written the book, was evidently unintended.

The NEA managed to deflect the criticism, kidding with some uninformed callers, for example, that Jong's book was about an astronaut. The important point, though, was that in the climate of the time, Erica Jong's sexual indiscretions weren't seen as justifying a major retrenchment in the NEA's program.

Another tense episode arose from the complaint of Congressman Mario Biaggi in 1984 that a performance of the Verdi opera *Rigoletto*, which the NEA had helped to fund, was insulting to Italians. An ad for the show featured a man dressed in black suit and white hat, emerging from large letters that spelled "RIGOLETTO." The letters were riddled with bullet holes. Biaggi wrote to then–NEA chair Frank Hodsoll, protesting the use of federal funds "to denigrate a particular ethnic group by promoting a stereotype," and demanding that the NEA dissociate itself from *Rigoletto*. Hodsoll responded that although he agreed the ad was "in poor taste," he could not interfere; the endowment's integrity depended on its "avoiding any appearance of attempting to influence or control artistic content."[5]

Biaggi then sought to amend the NEA law to ban the funding of productions containing "any ethnic or racially offensive material." In testimony before Congress, Hodsoll opposed the amendment.

He pointed out that government bureaucrats should not be in the business of telling an opera company how to interpret a great work of art. "To take any other approach would be to determine that there is only one officially accepted interpretation of 'Rigoletto,'" and that "only productions in keeping with this official state interpretation shall be funded."

Hodsoll added that any legally imposed ban on funding art that offends or stereotypes an ethnic group would be impossible to apply fairly, would likely lead to discrimination against classics "that might give offense to one or another group," and "would be subject to the most egregious form of arbitrary decisionmaking based on personal taste." Works that might be disqualified under an "ethnic stereotype" standard, Hodsoll said, include Tennessee Williams's *Streetcar Named Desire* (Poles) and Shakespeare's *Merchant of Venice* (Jews).[6] Representative Biaggi's proposal to censor the ideas found in NEA-supported works died a peaceful death.

Through the leadership of Hodsoll, the earlier NEA chair Nancy Hanks, and others, the endowment in its first twenty years managed to create a presence for live theater, classical music, dance, and the visual arts in cities and towns throughout America. The agency was able to do this through the catalytic effect of its grants, which usually required that matching funds be raised. Corporate contributions just seemed to flow once the NEA had given a project its approval.

Garrison Keillor, the writer and radio raconteur, wryly but lovingly described the achievements of the NEA in 1990:

> Today, in every city and state, when Americans talk up their home town, when the Chamber of Commerce puts out a brochure, invariably they mention the arts—a local orchestra or theater or museum or all three. It didn't used to be this way. Forty years ago, if an American man or woman meant to have an

artistic career, you got on the train to New York. Today, you can be a violinist in North Carolina, a writer in Iowa, a painter in Utah. This is a small and lovely revolution that the National Endowment has helped to bring about. . . . Today, no American family can be secure against the danger that one of its children may decide to become an artist. [7]

Then in 1989, somehow the system went awry. It's not altogether clear what made it happen; probably a number of factors combined.

First among these was the increasing power and visibility of America's fundamentalist right, which had helped elect Ronald Reagan and George Bush. The fundamentalist right-wing agenda stressed what it called "social" issues: sexuality, the proper place of women, patriotism, and religion, wrapping them all in highly charged rhetoric about preserving Judeo-Christian cultural values.

The fundamentalist challenge presented more than a conflict over values. For the message of religiously based "profamily" leaders like Donald Wildmon of the American Family Association or Pat Robertson of the Christian Coalition was not merely that *their* views on sexuality, women's rights, reproductive freedom, and religion were correct, but that other views should not even be heard. As John Frohnmayer, the embattled chair of the NEA from late 1989 to early 1992 observed, the battle was not so much over dirty words, nudity, or homosexuality; the "real debate is about the nature of tolerance . . . and the willingness of people to encounter differences."[8]

A second likely reason for the sensationalist pressures that beset the NEA from 1989 until at least the middle of 1992 had to do with the age-old problem of scapegoating speech for social ills. America was in a slump, facing dramatic social changes, and finding it difficult to face the reality of economic and political decline. Historically, periods of frustration or insecurity are breeding grounds for demagogues who distract attention from social problems by attacking artistic rebels and other dissenters, and by scapegoating symbols.

A third factor contributing to the political beating that the NEA endured in these years may have been simply antagonism on the part of many Americans toward "the arts" or "high culture." A long-standing popular American suspicion of "egghead" intellectuals was echoed in the frequent use of such stock political epithets as "East Coast liberals" or "cultural elites." Despite the success over the years of agencies like the NEA and the Corporation for Public Broadcasting in popularizing classical music, theater, and visual art, there's still a large gap in America between popular culture and high culture, a suspicion of artists whose work may be difficult, obscure or "avant-garde." Thus, fundamentalist leaders were able to generate thousands of letters and postcards to Congress, the White House, and the NEA protesting "pornography" or "blasphemy" in particular works of art that the protesters had not even seen, but knew of "only through the sensationalized [and distorting] filter of the media or direct mail fundraising campaigns."[9]

This "fear of art" made the NEA an appealing target, particularly when combined with the agency's job of promoting experiment and innovation. In fact, as the NEA controversy proceeded, it became increasingly apparent that the goal of many of the agency's critics was to abolish arts funding altogether.

Related to these social and cultural factors was the onset of what Columbia University Professor Carole Vance calls a "sex panic," a "political maneuver designed to bypass" the usual, rational defenses that might be mounted on behalf of art or social tolerance by stirring up fears and inhibitions—attitudes that sex is somehow "polluting, shameful and dangerous."[10] Sexuality, sexual inhibition, sexual guilt, shame, anxiety, repression—all are powerful human forces that can be harnessed for political ends.

Perhaps a final factor in explaining the explosion and persistence of the arts funding issue was the inability of the arts world to mount a unified defense or produce strong, defiant, eloquent, and credible spokespersons who could confidently put the demagogues in their place.

1989: Hot-button Issues and a Fine Slogan

As Donald Wildmon, head of the Tupelo, Mississippi-based American Family Association tells the story, it all started with a postcard from a constituent notifying him that an artwork called *Piss Christ* was hanging in a museum in North Carolina. The work in question was a large, luminous photograph of a crucifix immersed behind a shimmering reddish-gold liquid. Only the work's title suggested that the artist might have an ambivalent attitude toward the powerful Christian symbol at the center of the work.

Piss Christ was the work of Andres Serrano, a New York artist who had for years been exploring the meanings of sacred symbols. Serrano, a Catholic, was interested in the way these powerful symbols were cheapened and commercialized. He was also interested in the sacred and profane meanings of bodily fluids. In his art, he often incorporated these essential fluids—blood, semen, milk, urine—into his work. Previous experiments with body fluids had produced "gorgeous sunsetlike veils," "apocalyptic 'landscapes'" and "shadowy figures," sometimes "blend[ing] ideas of nourishment and pain in a single image."[11]

But Serrano's ambivalence and artistic intentions got badly lost in the row that followed. Critics said he *must* have known his title would offend devout Christians. Wildmon, Senator Jesse Helms, and others who claimed to represent true Christianity, lost no time in beating up a froth of righteous indignation over the "taxpayers" being "forced" to fund such purported insults to their faith.

Soon enough, another example of supposed NEA malfeasance was unearthed. The agency had helped fund a traveling retrospective exhibition of the works of the recently deceased, much celebrated, but unquestionably controversial American photographer, Robert Mapplethorpe. The subjects of Mapplethorpe's stunning photographs—as probably few Americans now need to be told—include not only gorgeous flowers and nudes but extremely large, lovingly photographed penises, and sadomasochistic sexual practices like dressing up in leather or urinating into another person's mouth.

One notorious Mapplethorpe photo was a self-portrait of the artist, bare ass in the foreground, face turned toward the camera with an expression that was at once both sad and mischievous, and bullwhip inserted firmly in his anus. Obviously, Mapplethorpe's intent was, in part, to confront—and force viewers to confront—the reality of some unusual sexual practices. This photo from Mapplethorpe's *X Portfolio* was a small part of the traveling exhibit, but it was pure gold for those who wanted to whip up indignation over "misuse of taxpayers' dollars."

There had always been a substantial body of opinion, mostly on the right wing of the political spectrum, that government had no business funding art. President Ronald Reagan, for example, had tried mightily to get rid of the NEA in his first term. Mapplethorpe and Serrano presented an ideal opportunity to advance this agenda.

"The taxpayers' money" was a perfect if misleading slogan for this crusade. The NEA's critics claimed that their complaints about some of the art that was funded and their insistence that tax monies not be spent on certain projects—those deemed sexually explicit, homoerotic, unpatriotic, or insulting to organized religion—did not amount to censorship. It was only that the government shouldn't *sponsor* such offensive works. Controversial artists could create controversial art on their own time and "with their own dime."

"Sponsorship, not censorship" became a popular refrain on innumerable talk shows and in countless newspaper columns. As one wag quipped, these may be "cutting-edge" artists, but they shouldn't expect the government to buy the scissors.

The "taxpayers" argument became almost irresistible: how could any legislator vote *against* the proposals of Jesse Helms and others to prevent the NEA from funding "obscene" or "indecent" art? How could one campaign for reelection faced with the inevitable opposition ad claiming that "Senator So-and-So voted for pornography tonight. Senator So-and-So wants to waste taxpayers' dollars so that you do not have enough money to buy your home. He wants that money to go on producing pornographic pictures of children, or people performing . . . unnatural sex acts"?[12]

"The taxpayers' money" became such a popular slogan that it was soon adopted by censors in other fields. Several parents in Waterloo, Iowa, objected in April 1992 to their school board's purchase of such purportedly indecent books as *The Handmaid's Tale, Lord of the Flies, Catcher in the Rye,* and *Of Mice and Men* for use in high school literature classes. One protester, complaining that the books contained profanity, lurid sex passages, and statements defamatory to minorities, God, women, and the disabled, urged parents to "let board members know we do not want our tax dollars spent on profanity and pornography."[13] Similarly, in Westminster, Maryland, a pressure group mounted a campaign to remove a book of short stories called *Jesus in the Mood* from the local public library.

The leader of the charge explained, "This is not a censorship thing. The public library is tax-supported and it should have some standard of moral decency."[14]

The Argument for Government Funding without Strings Attached

These attacks on the choices made by professional librarians dramatize one of the problems with the "taxpayers' money" slogan. For the "taxpayers" fund many things that individual citizens may not like—whether they be library book selections, school texts, public universities, savings and loan bailouts, foreign military adventures, or $600 toilet seats for advanced bombers. And usually the tab for these government activities is much higher than the NEA's measly (by federal government standards) $174 million per year (in 1992)— about 68 cents per American.

It's true that if taxpayers don't like something, they can protest, and maybe even get the funding decision reversed. Political unpopularity, after all, ultimately did end the Vietnam War, though it may never curb extravagant Pentagon expenditures. So why not try to influence the funding decisions of the NEA, the school board, or any other government body?

The reason why is that the stakes are different when it comes to government funding in the sensitive area of free expression. When a city, state, or federal government establishes and supports a public university, it's financing a "marketplace of ideas" (to use a tired but still-potent metaphor). It shouldn't expect that only those courses, books, and speeches that are favorable to the government or inoffensive to organized religion, the majority of Americans, or the majority of Christians, will be permitted. Such government-imposed ideological straitjackets would obviously hamper free inquiry, the very goal of a university. As the Supreme Court long ago recognized, the First Amendment "does not tolerate laws that cast a pall of orthodoxy over the classroom."[15]

The same is true when "the taxpayers" fund parks, sidewalks, or other public spaces given over to free speech activities. A city government isn't thought to sponsor every speaker, no matter how kooky, who makes use of public land. In fact, the opposite is true: it would be ideologically stifling, contrary to free speech values, and flatly unconstitutional for the government officials who operate these public spaces to impose tests of political correctness, acceptability, or inoffensiveness on those who seek to use the property.

The "taxpayers" who fund these open forums are not buying particular ideas that they like; they are buying one bigger idea— freedom. *All* the taxpayers help support a marketplace of ideas even though *some* of the particular ideas peddled at that market probably will not be to their liking. It's sort of a covenant that citizens share: we pool our tax money to support free speech, on the theory that we're a diverse society likely to be contentious and disagree. But free speech in public places is surely far better than letting the government decide what topics and viewpoints are permissible.

Because city, state, and federal agencies own so much property and support such varied educational and cultural activities, allowing ideological restrictions on creative expression that somehow benefits from government largesse would be particularly dangerous. It would, in essence, allow the government to accomplish indirectly what it cannot do directly: censor the ideas of the people.

There are many other examples of this principle. The federal government funds Fulbright scholarships for study abroad. Is every scholar so honored to produce only work approved by the government censors? Federal agencies fund science research grants. Are scientists to clear their conclusions with the government just because their work is supported by "taxpayers' money"? The postal service gives special rates and the Internal Revenue Service gives tax exemptions to nonprofit educational and charitable organizations. Are these diverse groups, espousing so many different causes, to receive these subsidies or benefits only if their books, ads, leaflets, and letters comply with government rules against "indecency" or "blasphemy"?

Arts funding is no different. The National Endowments for the Arts and Humanities, like the local university or library, and like tax-exempt schools and charities, are taxpayer-funded forums for free expression. The NEA is not the Voice of America, Radio Martí, or a presidential press conference—all of which use tax money for *government* expression. Instead, it's like a public library, college, museum, or municipal theater. These institutions receive tax money for the arts, but it's not expected that every taxpayer will enjoy or appreciate every resulting book or painting or poem or performance. The overall idea is that some of us will benefit from some pieces of it, and our neighbors will benefit from others.

In fact, much of the NEA's funding doesn't even go to specific programs. It goes to artists to give them the time and freedom to develop new projects, or to institutions that in the course of any year will make hundreds of separate choices about what to present, publish, or perform. Trust and freedom are essential ingredients of funding like this. Curators, editors, and theater directors can't have a bureaucrat looking over their shoulders with a checklist of offensive words, images, or subjects as they make each artistic decision, any more than a professor can teach, or a librarian can select books, with the likes of Senator Helms breathing down his or her neck or snooping around to detect whether there are any "subversive," "blasphemous," "indecent," or otherwise "offensive" ideas floating about.

In this sense, the way that funding for the Serrano and Mapplethorpe exhibits worked was typical. Serrano had been selected not by the NEA but by the Southeastern Center for Contemporary Art in North Carolina, to be one of ten artists included in a traveling show. The museum had received $75,000 in NEA money—about a quarter of the show's cost. Each of the ten artists was awarded $15,000.

Similarly, the University of Pennsylvania's Institute of Contemporary Art had received some NEA support for a Mapplethorpe retrospective. The choice of works to be included was left to the curators, not to the government. The curators felt that a full understanding of this talented, controversial artist required that his most shocking works, works documenting some extreme and disturbing sexual practices, be included.

The "taxpayers' money" argument sounds appealing, but it's lethal. If valid, it would mean that the NEA could decide to fund only art consistent with the platform of the dominant political party; only art inoffensive to Protestant Christian leaders (or to Catholic, Jewish, Buddhist, or atheist beliefs); only art that condemned homosexuality (or encouraged it, or simply expressed a note of toleration); only art that supported American foreign policy, didn't offend any religion, didn't promote (or even mention) Marxism (or fascism, or capitalism, or vegetarianism), didn't use the symbol of the American flag, didn't deal with sex—and so on.

It would be impractical, as well as intolerable, for arts funding to work in such an inquisitorial atmosphere. There isn't enough NEA staff, nor would they have the expertise about a particular artist, century, genre, or subject matter, to substitute their judgments for those of the editors, theater directors, curators, and others who make decisions about the details of a show or work that the NEA has agreed to help support.

But these details of how funding really works, and the need to keep the process clear of political grandstanding, got lost in the heat of the media blitz over Serrano and Mapplethorpe. By parading these two examples of alleged NEA irresponsibility, demagogues brilliantly exploited a combination of homophobia, the power of religious symbols, generalized insecurities about social change and fears about sex, suspicions about "high culture" or the avant-garde, and resentments about government waste of taxpayers' money. NEA arts funding—a minuscule portion of the federal budget— became a winning issue in the media, in Congress, and in the ever-intense competition among right-wing "profamily" groups for direct mail dollars.

The Obscenity Oath, the "Chocolate-Smeared Woman," and "General Standards of Decency"

It was in the midst of this ongoing battle that Congress, in two years' time, imposed two unprecedented ideological restrictions on arts funding. The first, enacted in 1989, barred the NEA from supporting any art that the agency "may consider obscene," including "depictions of sadomasochism, homoeroticism, the sexual exploitation of children, or individuals engaged in sex acts and which, taken as a whole, do not have serious literary, artistic, political or scientific value." (Senator Helms had tried but failed to include insults to religious beliefs in this list.)

John Frohnmayer, then the NEA chair, decided to implement the new restriction by requiring all grant recipients to sign a certification that they accepted it. This "obscenity oath," as it came to be known, propelled a number of artists, especially those old enough to remember the antisubversive loyalty oaths of the 1950s, to reject their NEA grants. Joseph Papp of the New York Shakespeare Festival was among them; so were Bella Lewitzky, director of a California dance company, and the directors of the Newport Harbor

Art Museum in California.

Lewitzky and Newport Harbor brought a successful legal challenge to the oath and the Helms Amendment. The federal court that invalidated the "may consider obscene" requirement said it was unconstitutionally vague and chilled the exercise of First Amendment rights. Grant recipients would feel obliged to steer clear of anything that the NEA, or one of its political critics, *might* feel was "obscene." Just because this was a funding program did not mean the government could impose any conditions it wanted, no matter how vague, indecipherable, or ideologically biased.

The storm did not abate, however. In early 1990 those hungry for more spicy news about sex—particularly about homosexuality, outrageous artists, and "waste of taxpayers' money"—found new targets for indignation. News leaked to the press in the spring of 1990 that the NEA's Solo Performance Artist peer panel had recommended eighteen grants to individual artists, among them three who were homosexual and used themes of gay experience and homophobic bigotry extensively in their work: Holly Hughes, Tim Miller, and John Fleck.

The fourth artist who was caught in this political maelstrom and ended up losing a peer panel–recommended grant because of provocative publicity was Karen Finley. Probably the best-known of the four, Finley is a powerful performer who sometimes removes her clothes and

> often places, dabs, smears, pours and sprinkles food on her body to symbolize the violation of the female characters whose tales she shrieks and whines on stage. It's not her sexuality but her emotional intensity that engages her audiences. . . . Her most recurrent themes are incest, rape, violence, alcoholism, suicide, poverty, homelessness, and discrimination.
>
> Karen Finley does on stage and in public what many of the

bravest performers practice only as exercises in the relative safety and privacy of acting classes. Her work is nearly always shocking and invariably—some would say relentlessly—political.[16]

In her 1990 piece, "We Keep Our Victims Ready," Finley "used her body as a canvas, smearing herself with chocolate, red candies, alfalfa sprouts, and tinsel to dramatize society's institutionalized debasement of women."[17] This particular segment of her art caught the mass media's attention, and Karen Finley became widely known simply as the "nude, chocolate-smeared woman." It was typical of the distortion and sensationalism that greeted these artists that the provocative epithet for Finley came to replace any real discussion about her work.

At the time that Finley, Hughes, Fleck, and Miller were being pilloried in the press, the NEA was facing the toughest congressional reauthorization battle of its life. Then–NEA chair John Frohnmayer felt himself to be under massive pressure to avoid controversial grants. Just days before Frohnmayer overruled the peer panel and publicly announced his denial of the recommended grants, he had received a note from President Bush deploring the "filth" purveyed by these artists, as described in a recent *Washington Times* article, and seeking assurance that such "filth and patently blasphemous material" would not be funded.

The four artists sued, challenging the legality of Frohnmayer's action. Shortly after that suit was filed, Congress passed its second restriction on NEA funding. This time, the NEA chair was instructed to make sure that all grants took into account "general standards of decency and respect for the diverse beliefs and values of the American public." The *Finley* v. *NEA* lawsuit was soon amended to challenge the constitutionality of this "decency" requirement.

The decency language had been seen as a good compromise in

some quarters. Senator Helms, Senator Alfonse D'Amato, and others had been pressing for more specific prohibitions. Some arts supporters thought that a decency standard was harmless, precisely because it was so vague. But its chilling effect soon became apparent: decency was a signal not only to the unpredictable Chairman Frohnmayer, who sometimes caved in to pressure and vetoed meritorious grants, but on other occasions eloquently defended controversial works. It was also a signal to artists that "indecent" work would not be tolerated. The fact that everyone has his or her own interpretation of what is indecent, and that indecent is not at all the same as legally obscene, only made the intimidation and uncertainty worse. Theater directors, literary magazine editors, art curators, and film festival planners could only guess what would be likely to raise another political storm, and could only err on the far side of anything having to do with sex or religion if they didn't want to get burned.

In June 1992 a federal court in the *Finley* case ruled that the decency requirement, like the "may be obscene" requirement before it, was unconstitutionally vague and hindered free expression. Even when the government is doing the funding, it can't wield its formidable power to exact ideological conformity. As Judge Wallace Tashima wrote:

> The fact that the exercise of professional judgment is inescapable in arts funding does not mean that the government has free rein to impose whatever content restrictions it chooses, just as the fact that academic judgment is inescapable in the university does not free public universities from First Amendment scrutiny. The right of artists to challenge conventional wisdom and values is a cornerstone of artistic and academic freedom.

Judge Tashima's ruling came at a political moment when the

NEA was more seriously compromised than ever. In February 1992 Republican presidential candidate Pat Buchanan ran campaign ads that accused George Bush of funding "pornographic" and "blasphemous" art "too shocking to show." In response, Bush finally fired Frohnmayer. Frohnmayer's departure took effect May 1, and within days his successor, acting chair Anne-Imelda Radice, was testifying before Congress that she would veto grants for any "sexually explicit" art or other projects that dealt with "difficult subject matter" or did not "appeal to the widest audience."

Radice's thinly veiled promises to toe the right-wing political line met a rueful response from Representative Sidney Yates, one of the congressmen who had supported the original NEA legislation. "This would seem to mark a change from the freedom and openness of John Frohnmayer and his predecessors," Yates said, apparently forgetting Frohnmayer's occasional deviations from artistic principle.

Within a week Radice fulfilled her promise to Congress by vetoing grants for two art exhibits that had been recommended by a peer panel and approved by the National Council on the Arts. The grants would have supported a show entitled *Corporal Politics* at the Massachusetts Institute of Technology's List Visual Arts Center, and another at Virginia Commonwealth University, also focusing on human body parts as symbols of alienation. Two peer panels subsequently decided not to complete their deliberations until Radice offered some reasoned explanation for her actions, and a number of groups, Beacon Press among them, declined NEA grants in protest. Composer Stephen Sondheim and author Wallace Stegner both turned down National Medal of the Arts awards in the wake of Radice's action. The rock group Aerosmith donated $10,000 to the List Center as a gesture of support. And playwright Jon Robin Baitz announced that he would donate an amount equal to his own recent NEA award to MIT and Virginia Commonwealth. Explaining his action, Baitz said:

> Being deemed politically acceptable by Chairwoman Radice is a dubious honor. It seems to be rather like being given the thumbs up by the Vichy government in France during the Second World War. . . .
>
> I will simply not be complicit with faux-moralist sharpies of the right, nor with psycho-sexual hysterics in the cultural sacking of this country, which has once again become a favorite conservative pastime.[18]

Government benefits are a fact of modern life. The NEA was critically compromised because of the fearful, censorious approach to funding decisions that it followed in the wake of relentless media sensationalism and fundamentalist attacks. The endowment took this beating because too many Americans either didn't care about defending controversial art or let themselves be persuaded by sensationalist and cynical "not with my tax money" rhetoric.

The good news is that "sex panics" do tend to subside; witch-hunts wear themselves out. But the damage they do may take years to repair. Rebuilding the NEA, and safeguarding the integrity of other government programs established to advance free expression will require a new commitment to experimentation, tolerance, and diversity, and a willingness to confront the unpleasant realities and shocking metaphors that artists sometimes deliver.

⊚ 7 ⊚

The Dreaded "P" Word: Pornography

*Acton, who was regarded a half century ago as the chief
English authority on sexual matters, declared that, "hap-
pily for society," the supposition that women possess sexual
feelings could be put aside as a "vile aspersion," while
another medical authority of the same period stated in
regard to the most simple physical sign of healthy sexual
emotion that it "only happens in lascivious women."*

—Havelock Ellis, *On Life and Sex*

HEN 1992 REPUBLICAN PRESIDENTIAL ASPIRANT PATRICK Buchanan wanted to push the two hottest buttons he could think of, he produced a TV ad accusing President Bush of using the National Endowment for the Arts to fund "blasphemy" and "pornography." When fundamentalist parents object to school text or library books containing information about sex, they complain about public funding of "pornography." The performance art of Karen Finley, the photographs of Robert Mapplethorpe—indeed, virtually any art with sexual content or even simple nudity—has been accused of being "pornography."

What does this dreaded P-word really mean? How did it get to be—at least in public discourse—such a frequent synonym for evil?

Pornography and Erotica

The word "pornography" was invented by a nineteenth-century art historian to describe the erotic paintings and statues found by archeologists a century earlier when they unearthed the ancient Italian cities of Herculaneum and Pompeii from the volcanic ashes that had buried them back in A.D. 79. Scientists and historians were alarmed to see the graphic depictions of sexual acts that had adorned the public places of these ancient cities, and their response was to lock the controversial frescos and statues inside a secret museum where women and children could not see them.[1]

"Pornography" comes from two Greek words: *porně*, meaning prostitute, and *grapho*, meaning writing. Presumably, prostitutes weren't writing, or being written about, for spiritual uplift but for sexual gratification. The dictionary definition of pornography is, therefore, simply writing or pictures "intended to arouse sexual desire."[2]

Pornography comes in almost as many varieties as the human sexual impulse, and though much of it is far from great art, pornographic works can also be funny, artistic, and even profound. The eighteenth-century best-seller *Memoirs of a Woman of Pleasure* (otherwise known as *Fanny Hill*) has undoubted literary value: it is a well-written social satire. The book is also classic pornography: a series of sexual episodes, written for libidinous arousal, strung along a loose plot line. As with any pornographic work, many readers no doubt rushed through the nonsexual connective passages to get to the next "good part."

Of course, readers, especially young ones, have also done this with works that *weren't* intended as pornographic, such as D. H. Lawrence's *Lady Chatterley's Lover*. Lawrence hated pornography, which he viewed as cheapening and vulgarizing the sanctity of sex.

The term "pornography" thus embraces a wide range of written and pictorial aphrodisiacs. It means something very different from obscenity, although the two words are often confused. "Obscenity" is a legal term for a category of sexually explicit art and entertainment that the Supreme Court has said is without First Amendment protection. According to those nine wise jurists, obscenity is sexually explicit material that lacks any serious artistic or other value, is patently offensive, and appeals to "shameful or morbid" sexual appetites, as judged by the standards of a particular community. Because pornographic works may arouse only healthy sexual urges, may have serious artistic value, and may not be considered patently offensive in a particular community, most pornography is not legally obscene.

Sometimes people try to distinguish between pornography (naughty, ugly, no redeeming value, leering or prurient in character) and erotica (nice, arty, more upper-class, not prurient but open and wholesome). A small subgroup of feminists define pornography as violent or "degrading" sexual material; work that's nonviolent, or without themes of dominance and submission, is erotica. In short, pornography is anything with sexual content that you disapprove of; erotica is sexual material that's okay.

These distinctions are hard to maintain; for one thing, they're terribly subjective. To paraphrase a famous Supreme Court case, one person's literary masterpiece may be another's smutty trash. "It is largely because government officials cannot make principled distinctions in this area that the Constitution leaves matters of taste and style so largely to the individual."[3]

The images and stories described or acted out in pornography are sexual fantasies that turn people on. *What* turns people on is a complicated question; our sexual responses are in large part biological, but are also conditioned by social experiences and associations.

There is much that's sexist, misogynist, and violent in our society and all of it is reflected in our sexual fantasies and in pornography.

Pornography is created by people—individual men and women—whose fantasies and inspirations are in turn products both of their humanity and of the society in which they live. Social conventions, family dynamics, childhood experiences, and powerful taboos all influence our adult sexual imaginings. "How much of any particular feature of our sexuality can be traced to environmental causes, how much to hard-wired biology, and how much to a cross-reaction between the two, seems unanswerable in nearly every case."[4]

Pornography in all its variety is a creation of our bodies and minds—sometimes a reflection of impulses that we prefer to repress, or that law and social custom repress for us. If, for example, some small fraction of society's hard-core pornography reflects violent rape fantasies (as does a fraction of nonpornographic entertainment), that's because such myths and fantasies do exist, in society and perhaps in our biology as well. It's the *impulses* that, if not contained, cause people to act—not their written or filmed reflections.

Pornography in visual art began with the ancients. From African art to Greek antiquities, images of erect phalluses abound. The satyr, a familiar figure in Greek mythology, is pictured often; almost always with an impressive erection.

Sexuality has also been a staple of Eastern art, the erotic religious sculptures of India being one vivid example. Among the many treasures of pornographic Asian art is Hokusai's *Dream of the Fisherman's Wife*, which depicts an attentive octopus caressing a blissful nude woman with all of its tentacles, while also studiously performing cunnilingus. A sex manual from first-century China called *The Art of the Bedchamber* described female homosexuality and masturbation in elaborate detail.[5]

Not just nudity and sex, but scenes of torture, sadomasochism, flagellation, bestiality (especially if one considers satyrs beasts), and rape in classical art are virtually numberless. Such sexually charged works are found in major museums all over the world; many of them have explicitly religious themes. Sexuality, masochism, and religious ecstacy are all mixed together in Western art, as they are in Western culture.

The seventeenth-century Flemish master Peter Paul Rubens painted many erotic scenes, including lesbian lovers; the French painter Courbet did him one better with his famous *Sleepers*—two naked women, their legs lazily wrapped around each other in the blessed relaxation of postorgasmic sleep. Rembrandt's erotic works include a monk and nun making love in a cornfield, also a couple enjoying themselves famously in a big Dutch bed (the woman has three arms!).

Pornography flourished in both nineteenth-century literature and painting. "The oft-ogled American pinup girl," according to one critic, "has a deeply rooted, if perhaps surprising, geneology, with a point of origin in certain pictorial conventions of late 19th century academic painting." These "establishment" painters created

> a seemingly endless series of prurient female images: Andromedas in Victorian versions of handcuffs; Salomes strip-dancing before the severed head of John the Baptist; Venuses rolling in their birth waves; female personifications of Hope (kinkily blind-folded), Temptation (often with one breast wantonly exposed), and Virtue (ironically stark naked). Indeed, what emerged was a high-flown prototype of soft-core pornography itself, in which women operated as fantasies in the newly emerging—and newly heterosexual—pornographic imagination.[6]

These common pornographic images—scantily clad women in distress, women admiring themselves in mirrors, women somehow bound or restrained—all have their roots in Western European painting and literature. It's worth remembering, though, that the sexual fantasies reflected in these images are not necessarily acted out in real life. Probably many such fantasies don't even represent desires. They may instead (like the fairy tales that children find so compelling) be mental reruns of old or archetypal fears.

It's not easy to untangle why violence and sex are linked in some sexual fantasies, and therefore in some pornography. The reasons these fantasies are so common in our culture may have to do with our social and family structure. That is, as one psychotherapist explains, sexual role-playing involving dominance and submission may be rooted in childhood psychological needs, especially for men, to separate from all-powerful nurturing mothers.[7]

Maybe it won't always be so. Artists and writers today are producing pornography that's neither brutal nor coercive nor degrading to any of the participants. According to various estimates, violent pornography (that is, work depicting rape or sadomasochism) today accounts for only 3–8 percent of the available material. Most male-oriented commercial porn focuses not on violence but simply on depictions of willing and lusty (and therefore available) women.[8]

It's true that most of the pornographic images that have come down to us from long tradition have been intended for the gratification of heterosexual males. But this isn't necessarily a reason to try to wipe out the whole genre, as has been suggested by fundamentalists and even some feminists. Pornography served males because *all* of society served males: government, religion, law, domestic relationships. Pornography reflected but did not create male domination any more than any other form of art or literature did. With social advances—women's liberation and gay rights—we are already seeing more variety in pornography.

What may be new about pornography in the twentieth century is its hard-core variety. The invention of photography made it possible to document nature, including human behavior, with a kind of graphic accuracy that today includes such technical wonders as "cum shots" and close-ups of sexual penetration.[9] However inartful, even unerotic, this sort of documentation may seem, showing in glorious (or clinical) detail how people behave sexually and what our bodies look like up close is not obviously wrong. As one writer has pointed out,

> Pornography is the one arena that is not afraid of the penis, even when erect, that does not find sperm disgusting, that shows pictures of men ejaculating in slow motion, even as other films emphasize the beauty of birds flying or dolphins leaping. And it is in the world of pornography where much of traditional male hatred and fear of vaginas has been redirected toward vaginal appreciation, through what writer Michael Hill calls "graphic and realistic depictions of the cunt as beautiful, tasty, wonderful to smell and touch."[10]

Not all pornography is artful; little of it is very edifying. But the question remains, does sexually arousing material cause any real harm? Does it do any good? Is there any reason why those who benefit from pictorial, or written, sexual aids shouldn't have access to them?

Psychologists recognize that pornography can aid in treating sexual dysfunctions, or simply in helping married couples liven up sagging sex lives.[11] Gay pornography has been helpful to many men and women both as a turn-on and in validating their sexual orientation. One therapist and sex educator has written:

As a board-certified clinical sexologist, I can tell you that it is common knowledge in my field that sexually explicit films and videos are often recommended as a mode of treatment for couples or individuals with clinical sexual problems. Such materials are viewed professionally as helpful, not harmful, assets in the treatment process.[12]

The American public seems to agree. Videos from the adult shelf now account for some 15–30 percent of overall rentals—about 410 million adult videos rented in 1991. Women, either singly or in couples, comprise more than 40 percent of those renting adult movies.[13]

The Politics of Pornography

Despite pornography's longevity and popularity, despite its widely varying quality and subject matter, and despite its therapeutic value, some Americans would nevertheless like to ban it. This opposition to sexually arousing material may come from a number of sources: religious beliefs; attitudes about sexual morality or the sexuality of women; ideological objections to the idea of casual or promiscuous sex; anger at perceived misogynist or violent messages in some commercial porn (messages that are also found, of course, in many mainstream movies, books, ads, and TV shows). Some Americans are offended by particular types of pornography that depict what they view as nonconformist behavior: gay or lesbian sex, oral or anal intercourse, sadomasochistic games, and so forth.

There's no question that images and scenes in pornography can feel profoundly threatening. Pornography has always explored sexual practices beyond the routine or conventional. Certainly, the activities portrayed in pornography go well beyond anything necessary for procreation. Religious leaders who view sex as only appropriate for reproduction are therefore likely to disapprove of words and images that promote sexual pleasure for its own sake. Likewise, religions and philosophies that preach repression of physical gratification in favor of spiritual fulfillment (whether in this life or the next) may object to porn on ideological grounds.

The quarrel with pornography, though, goes beyond the fact that some offerings explore the outer reaches, or less-traveled pathways, of human sexuality. Some opponents object to the depiction even of missionary-position sex. They may feel that it's too private a matter—that sex simply shouldn't be discussed. Or they may think that the celebration of sexual pleasure in pornography loosens the social restraints they view as essential for a well-ordered, productive society.

It's worth noting that those who would suppress pornography often betray a mighty fascination with the subject of their condemnation. In 1990, Donald Wildmon's American Family Association reproduced portions of artworks that it viewed as scandalously homoerotic, then mailed them by the truckload to its membership list, with a fund appeal letter noting that if contributions were sent, the AFA would supply more of this awful stuff. A 1992 Christian Coalition newsletter described in juicy detail a lesbian film that it simultaneously excoriated the NEA for having funded.

A similar scenario was played out more than twenty years ago when U.S. senators eager to drive the liberal Justice Abe Fortas from the Supreme Court mounted a campaign against him based on his votes in obscenity cases. The feature of the campaign was a "Fortas Obscene Film Festival," concocted out of some of the movies that Fortas, during his time on the Court, had voted were not obscene within the meaning of the law. This senatorial peep show was exceedingly popular among those most vociferously opposed to pornography.[14]

It's probably not exaggerating the point to suggest that some among the self-righteous who condemn pornography are denying their own sexual impulses, whether consciously or not. This clipping from the March 1991 *New York Times* is typical:

ANTI-PORNOGRAPHY PROSECUTOR
IS CHARGED WITH SEX OFFENSE

ST. LOUIS, MARCH 12. The chief state prosecutor for the city of St. Louis, who has spent most of his 15 years in office crusading against obscenity, pornography and prostitution, was charged today with a misdemeanor offense of patronizing a prostitute.

After initially denying a report on the matter . . . , the prosecutor, George Peach, acknowledged today that he tried to solicit sex from an undercover police officer Tuesday night at a motel.

Since being elected as circuit attorney in 1976, Mr. Peach has led a fight to rid St. Louis of pornography and prostitution. In the 1980s he was responsible for closing the city's major pornographic book and video stores. Last June he endorsed changes in city ordinances that would make jail mandatory for prostitutes, pimps and customers who are second time offenders.

On the other side of the pornography/censorship debate are those who view repressed sexuality as dangerous, and sexual fulfillment not only as our God-given right but as essential to healthy, productive, and satisfying lives. They point out that little that's found in pornography today isn't also covered—although often more tastefully—in such mainstream sex manuals as *The Joy of Sex*. And although orthodox Christianity has traditionally condemned almost all sexual practices except intercourse for reproductive purposes, other religions view sexual congress as sacred and don't draw the sharp distinction between physical and spiritual gratification that Judeo-Christian culture does. India's *Kama Sutra*, though sometimes found in the "Sex and Marriage" section of bookstores, is also a religious work.

That so much of the opposition to pornography is driven by religious orthodoxies suggests just how political this controversy is. Ideas about sexual experimentation and abandon, sex solely for physical gratification, and sex without emotional commitment may be profoundly threatening to established institutions. The idea that women are fully as sexual as men, with impulses, responses, and fantasies as powerful as men's, was politically heretical not so long ago, and in some circles still is so. (See, for example, the quotation that opens this chapter.) "Pornography is still the medium that most vociferously advocates free and diverse sexual expressiveness, a radical stance in our culture, which is still essentially puritanical and sex-negative."[15]

Pornography, then, conveys many political messages. That's why it's been such a ready target in the culture wars. Religious right crusaders link pornography, whether correctly or not, with increases in sexual freedom, reproductive rights, gay rights, divorce, and other signs of what they view as declining morality, the "separation of sexual pleasure from reproduction, marriage, and traditional family life."[16] Yet it's precisely because the content and ideas in pornography are controversial that it is so important to defend the First Amendment rights of those who produce and enjoy sexually arousing art.

The Attack on Pornography: How Sex Got to Be a Dirty Word

In 1967 President Lyndon Johnson appointed a panel of experts to study the issue of pornography and the operation of American obscenity laws. After three years of intensive research, the National Commission on Obscenity and Pornography found no evidence that pornography was harmful; the real problem, it said in its 1970 report, was "the inability or reluctance of people in our society to be open and direct in dealing with sexual matters."[17] The commission called for the repeal of existing obscenity laws, except those concerning children. Contemporaneous studies in Denmark and Britain reached the same conclusions.

In 1985, President Reagan's attorney general, Edwin Meese, convened another commission, saying that "re-examination of the issue of pornography is long overdue." The Meese Commission's agenda was clear: to discredit the conclusions of the 1970 commission as a way of justifying stepped up obscenity prosecutions, harsh new laws, and other strategies for wiping out as much sexually oriented art and entertainment as possible.

The Meese Commission was chaired by a zealous antipornography prosecutor named Henry Hudson, and heavily weighted with people whose minds were made up on the subject. Its executive director, Alan Sears, had forged a legal career devoted to censoring sexual content in art; Sears went on to become legal counsel for Charles Keating's right-wing Citizens for Decency Through Law. One commissioner, Park Dietz, declared that TV programs like *Miami Vice* and *Hunter* were "the most harmful form of pornography."[18]

Any pretense of impartiality dissolved as the Meese Commission hearings degenerated into a parade of witnesses recounting stories of sexual abuse by men who they said had been inspired by pornography. The complex sources of abusive, often criminal behavior by seriously dysfunctional individuals were now reduced to the simplistic explanation: "Porn made them do it." At the end, the commission issued a bulky two-volume report, much of it consisting of detailed narrations of the plots of pornographic movies, dutifully set down by FBI agents who'd been assigned to view them—at taxpayers' expense, of course.

Although admitting that the scientific evidence was inconclusive, the commissioners (over two dissents) announced that this evidence, plus their own common sense, led them to believe that pornography caused sexual crimes. They ignored all evidence to the contrary, including a recent study by the U.S. government's own surgeon general that found no link between pornography and violence. Social scientists whose studies the commission had cited publicly protested that their conclusions had been misrepresented. One called the Meese Commission's misuse of his data "bizarre."[19]

One of the Meese Commission's many recommendations was to create a special antipornography unit in the U.S. Department of Justice. This unit would bring more and harsher obscenity prosecutions, encourage and coordinate prosecutions by local U.S. attorneys and state district attorneys, and develop other strategies to drive producers of libidinous material out of business. The goal, quite explicitly, was to remove as much erotic literature as possible from the marketplace, regardless of whether it was likely to be found legally obscene.

One means toward this end had already been suggested in 1985 by Brent Ward, then the U.S. Attorney in Utah. In 1985 Ward sent a letter to Meese urging that the government start obscenity investigations and prosecutions against distributors of sexually oriented material in different parts of the country simultaneously. This technique of simultaneous multiple prosecutions would be likely to drive distributors out of business, regardless of whether any conviction was actually obtained, because of the cost and burdens of legal defense. If the threat of multiple prosecutions wasn't enough to force distributors out of business, the government could keep harassing them until it eventually got a conviction somewhere.

Ward's strategy was adopted, and it worked. Within the next several years, more than a dozen distributors were forced to sign "plea agreements" promising that, in exchange for radically reduced criminal charges, they would not distribute *any* sexually oriented materials in the future. These included magazines such as *Playboy* and *Penthouse*, and books like *The Joy of Sex*, all of which the Justice Department acknowledged had full First Amendment protection and could not be considered obscene.

Meanwhile, our government's National Obscenity Enforcement Unit was busy sponsoring and attending conferences and training sessions cosponsored and cotaught by religious fundamentalists and private antipornography groups. According to FBI agents who worked with them, this Department of Justice unit, and particularly its leadership, were "religious zealots" who were on a crusade to wipe out all sexually arousing literature, and who had lost all sense of the distinction between legal obscenity and constitutionally protected talk and art about sex.[20] (See Chapter 1 for discussion of the legal lines the Supreme Court has drawn to protect art and other speech about sex while maintaining the obscenity exception to the First Amendment.) By 1992, three different federal courts had condemned the Justice Department's strategies, calling them bad-faith attempts to suppress First Amendment rights.

Yet the assault went on, and pornography continued to be a hot political issue in the legislature and the media. The U.S. Justice Department, "prodecency" activists, and major fundamentalist organizations such as Donald Wildmon's American Family Association and Charles Keating's Citizens for Decency Through Law continued to trumpet scientifically unsupported claims about a causal link between pornography and criminal behavior.

The Causation Issue, Or "Porn Made Me Do It"

Despite the frequency and vehemence of the claims made by pro-censorship forces, there is no credible scientific evidence that pornography causes men to commit rape or any other sexual crime. The only definite known result of reading or watching pornography is sexual excitement, often followed by masturbation. If anything, this release of sexual tension probably reduces the chances that an unstable individual might commit a sexual assault.[21]

Advocates of censorship generally point to four different types of "evidence" to bolster their claims that pornography actually causes crimes. First, they rely on Ted Bundy–style "confessions." Bundy was a psychopathic serial killer who sadistically murdered numerous college women before he was finally caught, tried, and executed by the State of Florida. In an interview shortly before his death, Bundy claimed that a steady diet of porn had made him do it.

But Bundy's literary tastes were wide-ranging. He was an avid collector of cheerleader magazines and reportedly stoked his fantasies with promotional materials from cheerleader camps and even illustrations in a college physiology textbook. Bundy was also a classic dissembler and a psychopath—not exactly the most credible witness.

The causes of criminal behavior are complex. Alcoholism, drug abuse, physical abuse, family dysfunction, and mental pathology are some of the factors that contribute to crime, including sexual crime. Sexual pathologies usually have their roots in childhood; they can't be created by movies and books. Most sex offenders come from sexually repressed and punitive homes, not the reverse;[22] while societies where children are exposed to sexuality have been found to experience less in the way of rape or other sexual violence.[23]

Second, antiporn crusaders claim that studies have found correlations between rape statistics and the availability of pornographic literature in a particular place. Or they say police departments have reported that a majority of sex offenders had pornography in their cars or homes.

Often these claims are just plain wrong. One "study" often cited by antipornography activists, for example, has been said to show that pornography was involved in 41 percent of sex crimes investigated by the Michigan State Police. Author Marcia Pally interviewed the state police officer responsible for maintaining criminal profiles, who told her no such study existed. The 41 percent statistic, he said, came from a 1977 master's thesis written by a student with a strongly religious bias; the student was "trying to establish causality, but as you know, you cannot establish causality between sexually explicit materials and sex crimes. We'd make a better causality case for alcohol." The officer added: "Our name got attached to the study about ten years ago—I don't know why. . . . Please tell everybody that we did no such study."[24]

Actual studies tend, on the contrary, to show that availability of sexually explicit material correlates with open and egalitarian societies, and with *less*, not more, sexual crime. This was the conclusion of research done in Denmark, Sweden, and West Germany after laws against pornography were scrapped.[25] By contrast, highly authoritarian societies, where women have little equality, often have virtually no commercial pornography available yet experience a high level of violence against women (this is true of Iran and Saudi Arabia, although the phenomenon is hardly limited to Islamic countries). The strongest argument, though, is the glaring fact that rigidly patriarchal societies treated women miserably and abusively long before the modern pornography industry existed.

On the other hand, Japan, where some of the most violent pornography is freely available, has a relatively low rate of assault against women. It is social and cultural conditioning that makes the difference.

More important, there's a vast difference between a "correlation" and a cause. A correlation between crime rates and the availability of

certain types of books or movies in a particular geographic area may
be mere coincidence, or it may be independently caused by a third
variable, such as the percentage of young males living in the vicinity.
There may be a "correlation" between beer-drinking, or blue
jean–wearing, and crime, but that doesn't mean that Budweiser
should be outlawed or The Gap put out of business.

One study that is often miscited by procensorship groups did
find a "correlation" of sorts between rape rates and availability of
sexually explicit material. The authors of the study determined that
no conclusion could be drawn; both rape rates and sales of pornography were actually driven by independent factors such as "hyper-
masculine" cultural attitudes and the resident population of males
between the ages of eighteen and twenty-four.

Sale of sexually oriented magazines does correlate with more
gender equality in a given area, however. That may be because both
equality and free speech tend to flourish where attitudes are more
tolerant.[26]

A third type of "evidence" cited by those who would censor
pornography are laboratory studies of male college students, which
allegedly show that prolonged exposure to sexually arousing materials causes an increase in aggressiveness, as measured in artificial
laboratory behavior like delivering an electric shock. These are the
same studies that the Meese Commission relied on, despite protests
from scientists that their works were being distorted and misused.

The most that any lab studies have actually been able to show
is that some male students, after intense exposure to *violent* pornography *and* after being deliberately angered, may act aggressively by
delivering an electric shock to a person who had previously antago-
nized them. These effects have only been found where the sexually
arousing material is violent; most pornography is not. Scientists say
that it's the violence, not the sex, that may arouse some subjects to

aggression in a lab setting. In this sense, as they point out, there is far more gratuitous violence in TV and R-rated movies than in pornography.

In addition, as the researchers acknowledge, laboratory results simply can't be translated to real-world behavior. Electric shocks administered in a lab are far different from sexual crimes, and the subjects know it. There are many factors (desire not to go to jail, for one) that inhibit people from committing actual crimes: they may well do things in a lab setting, where they know it's allowed, perhaps even expected, that they wouldn't ever do in real life. As the leading researchers have put it: "the use of artificial measures of aggression" in lab settings "prohibit direct extrapolation of experimental findings to situations outside the laboratory."[27]

The fourth, and in some ways most insidious, type of "evidence" used to argue for banning pornography is that it creates or reinforces bad attitudes. There are some laboratory studies that seem to suggest a steady diet of pornography can "desensitize" young men to the seriousness of sexual crimes. Of course, many other messages in popular entertainment, including Calvin Klein ads or a steady diet of Indiana Jones movies, might have the same effect.

One striking aspect of these attitude studies is that they show how callous attitudes toward rape or sexual violence can be rapidly changed by education and discussion ("debriefing"). In several studies where exposure to violent material was followed by debriefing, the male research subjects indicated less acceptance of the myth that women really want to be raped after participation in the experiment than they did before they walked into the room. Two of the leading researchers have concluded from the successes of debriefing that programs to discredit rape myths should become a standard part of sex education, for they "would go a long way toward countering the impact" of sexist and violent images throughout our culture.[28]

The idea of banning a category of art or entertainment because it fosters bad attitudes is chilling. Attitudes are caused by so many different factors that influence us over so long a period of time that to try to isolate one—one that can be a form of creative expression, no less—and then blame it for a massive, complex social problem like violence against women, verges on the irrational. It is also, at bottom, an escapist and totalitarian response. Only in totalitarian societies does government try to control behavior by controlling thoughts. If we start down this road, imposing censorship of the arts, the media, or any other form of expression because they reflect or reinforce bad attitudes, there wouldn't be enough censorship boards to go around.

Besides, it would be difficult to get a group as diverse as the American population to agree on what bad attitudes were. Some might name promiscuous sex; others would point to mindless hyperpatriotism; some would say atheism, others religious fanaticism. Some Americans might name tolerance of homosexuality as the chief evil, others, homophobia. The bottom line is that we can't give government the power to suppress ideas or attitudes because they're "dangerous."

The causation argument against pornography is fundamentally an argument that blames words and images for the acts of sick individuals. Criminal behavior generally has its roots in early life, and may be triggered by a virtually limitless range of stimuli: mainstream movies, TV shows, articles of clothing, newspaper crime reports. Would-be assassin John Hinckley claimed to be inspired by the movie *Taxi Driver*; mass murderer Charles Manson cited the Beatles' *White Album* and the Book of Revelation. The point is that the pathology has origins independent of whatever visual or written stimulus a sick person may find to feed it. As a committee established by the British government in the 1970s to study pornography observed, even "material dealing with bizarre and perverted sexual activity appeals only to those with a pre-existing interest established by the experiences of early life."[29]

An unstable individual could be "inspired" to commit a crime by a documentary on the evils of torture, an *anti*pornography tract like the Meese Commission Report, or writer Andrea Dworkin's turgid tome on the subject—the latter two containing lurid descriptions of the material they condemn. Much of the world's great art and literature describes, depicts, protests, or comments on sex, violence, or crime. The examples are endless, and range from Dostoevsky's great religious novel *Crime and Punishment*, to Titian's painting *The Rape of Europa* or Rubens's *The Rape of the Daughters of Leucippis*, to popular, timely, and thought-provoking films like *Thelma and Louise* or *The Accused*.

If words and pictures are to be blamed for the behavior of unstable individuals, we might as well start by outlawing the Bible. That good book has probably been cited as inspiration or justification for crime more frequently than any other text in Western history, from the inquisitions, witch-burnings, and pogroms of earlier eras to child abuse and ritual murders today. As one writer puts it, "If the state can ban pornography because it 'causes' violence against women, it can also ban *The Wretched of the Earth* because it causes revolution, *Gay Community News* because it causes homosexuality, *Steal This Book* because it causes thievery, and *The Feminine Mystique* because it causes divorce."[30]

Women and Pornography, Or Are There Politically Correct Sexual Fantasies?

Among those who want to ban pornography are some who identify themselves as feminists. The most prominent among them are probably law professor Catharine MacKinnon and writer Andrea Dworkin.

MacKinnon and Dworkin believe that pornography is a major source and cause of women's oppression; it's inherently coercive and degrading. They argue that boys and men are molded by, and act on, the ideas they see in pornography. Even if pornographic material doesn't actually *incite* sexual harassment and violence against women, the attitudes it promotes (for example, the idea that women like to be "fucked," dominated, or even raped) eventually lead men to such behavior. In the words of one pioneer feminist who has since, incidentally, rejected the censorship approach: "pornography is the theory; rape is the practice."[31]

These antiporn crusaders go one step further. They say that degrading images and ideas in pornography are not really just images and ideas; they actually *are* discrimination against women. Art substitutes for action and should be punished as if it were action. In other words, actually doing something about injustice is replaced by stamping out symbols of injustice.

MacKinnon and Dworkin confuse the images in pornography with actual sexual abuse because they mistakenly believe that all women are coerced into performing in pornography; none would do so voluntarily. Their assumption insults women who work in adult entertainment, both the producing and acting ends of the business, many of whom have spoken out eloquently about their choices. There is even a growing branch of pornography that sees itself as explicitly feminist.

This is hardly to say that no woman has ever been forced to perform in pornography. Where such crimes occur, both criminal and civil remedies should be aggressively pursued. Economic improvements—better job opportunities, expanded drug treatment, support for battered women—would also do much to give women involved in pornography (or prostitution) help, support, and viable alternatives. Campaigning for these reforms is something all feminists should be able to agree on, and would be a far more productive use of feminist energy than trying to stamp out pornography and thereby deny the rights not only of women who seek information and fantasy material about sex but women who choose a lifestyle of "sexual adventure."

MacKinnon and Dworkin have proven themselves brilliant organizers and publicists. They have captured a considerable following, especially among women discouraged by the intractable problems of sexual violence and abuse, and eager for simple, emotionally gratifying solutions. As one observer has recognized, MacKinnon's and Dworkin's appeal is essentially religious: their emotionally charged rhetoric is the language of religious conversion.[32]

Occasionally it becomes clear that MacKinnon's and Dworkin's fundamental complaint is the nature of sexual intercourse itself. They see even consensual heterosexual activity as violent and degrading. As MacKinnon has written, rape and intercourse "express the same power relation"; "sexuality is itself violating"; pornography is bad because it shows that women "desire to be fucked," "love to be taken and violated."[33] In this seductive but logically sloppy progression of words, being "fucked" (that is, having intercourse) is equated with being "taken" (an ambiguous term that doesn't necessarily connote violence), and with being "violated"—a term that unambiguously suggests rape. Similarly, Andrea Dworkin writes, "Fucking is an act of possession—simultaneously an act of ownership, taking, force; it is conquering. . . . The woman is acted on; the man acts and through action expresses sexual power."[34] Apart from its inherent subjectivity, this description reflects a singularly narrow and unimaginative view of the varied experiences of both men and women in sexual intercourse.

MacKinnon criticizes not only heterosexual intercourse but sexual liberation and abortion rights. In her view, such advances only make women more sexually available to men.[35]

Catharine MacKinnon is no mean intellect, and her contributions to feminism, particularly to the understanding of sexual harassment, have been considerable. But her attempts to suppress any ideas that don't conform to her sexual ideology are profoundly misguided. MacKinnon and Dworkin are dangerous because they are ideological totalists, refusing to accept any deviation from their concept of correct sexuality—or correct sexual fantasies. In this they resemble the fundamentalists of the right with whom they find themselves politically allied.

In 1983, the MacKinnon-Dworkin team drafted a model antipornography ordinance that differed radically from existing obscenity laws. The model ordinance created a "cause of action" (a right to sue) to ban the production, sale, distribution, or exhibition of any work of pornography, defined as "the graphic sexually explicit subordination of women, whether in pictures or in words," if any of a series of other criteria are met. These criteria included the presentation of women "dehumanized as sexual objects"; "in postures of sexual submission, servility, or display"; "being penetrated by objects"; "in scenarios of degradation"; or "as whores by nature"; or the exhibition of "women's body parts . . . such that women are reduced to those parts."

Each definitional term in this proposal is highly subjective. MacKinnon and Dworkin themselves have described simple intercourse as "subordination" or "sexual submission." A demonstration of the use of a speculum in a women's health guide fits within the criterion of women "being penetrated by objects." Feminist art that celebrates vaginal imagery, like Judy Chicago's *Dinner Party* or the paintings of Georgia O'Keeffe, arguably "reduces" women to their body parts. And what constitutes "degradation," or depicts women as "whores by nature" (*Madame Bovary*? *Ulysses*?) is of course very much in the mind of the beholder.

The MacKinnon-Dworkin proposal also created a legal right to sue for crime victims who claimed that pornography caused their assailant to attack them. This theory—of making artists, producers, and distributors liable for crimes supposedly inspired by their work—is one of these censors' most chilling contributions to the culture wars. It has inspired a series of bizarre legislative proposals, including, in 1991 and 1992, the federal "Pornography Victims Compensation Act" (sometimes also known as the "Bundy Bill"), which would give victims of sexual crimes the right to sue producers and sellers of sexually explicit material for unlimited money damages, on the theory that such material caused the criminal to commit the assault.

The MacKinnon-Dworkin model ordinance was first introduced in Minneapolis, Minnesota. Backed by a coalition of right-wing feminists and antipornography activists, the proposed ordinance passed the City Council, only to be vetoed by the mayor, who correctly believed it to be unconstitutional. After other abortive attempts, the ordinance finally passed in Indianapolis, Indiana, in 1984.

The American Booksellers Association and other literary trade groups promptly challenged the Indianapolis law, arguing that it was horrifically vague, imposed an ideological orthodoxy on erotic literature, and provided a means to suppress much expression that was constitutionally protected. A coalition of anticensorship feminist scholars and activists filed a lengthy friend-of-the-court brief detailing the many ways that censoring information and art about sex harms rather than helps women.

The Indiana federal court struck down the ordinance, and both the court of appeals and the Supreme Court affirmed its decision.

These courts agreed that, unlike obscenity laws, Indianapolis's ordinance singled out material for condemnation based on disapproval of its viewpoint—presumed advocacy of the sexual subordination of women. Viewpoint discrimination—government action that's aimed at the suppression of allegedly dangerous ideas — is among the gravest of First Amendment violations that a government can commit because it imposes ideological orthodoxy on citizens.

As some observers have noted, if misogyny is the true enemy, then most of mass entertainment is guilty, as well as much of world literature. If we are to eliminate misogyny through censorship, the first target should probably be the Bible, "for there could be no more explicit license extended to misogyny and the subordination of women than can be found in the Epistles of St. Paul."[36]

Although MacKinnon and Dworkin have captured a great deal of media attention, they do not represent the views of most women, including most feminists. Coalitions of anticensorship feminists have opposed the Indianapolis ordinance, the Bundy Bill, and other attempts to suppress erotic art, no matter how it's defined. They argue that while bad messages in pornography should be confronted and criticized, sexually arousing material is not necessarily degrading to women. On the contrary, women's sexual drives, both gay and straight, should be recognized and celebrated.

Anticensorship feminists recognize that there is a big difference between fantasy and action. In the realm of the imagination, especially the sexual imagination, it's hard to be politically correct.

By demonizing the images and ideas in pornography, the faction of right-wing feminists led by MacKinnon and Dworkin have done a great disservice to women. They have diverted energy and attention from real-world battles to symbolic ones. Instead of fighting actual discrimination at school or on the job, actual inadequacies in support for rape victims or prosecution of rapists and spouse batterers, actual lack of child care or child support enforcement, women are told to direct their energies toward stamping out pornography.

It's hard to calculate how much this distraction has cost the cause of women's rights. But one result is easy to spot: the "unholy alliance"[37] between these feminists and the religious right. Procensorship politicians and powerful fundamentalist organizations have adopted MacKinnon's and Dworkin's arguments, papering over their own profoundly nonegalitarian approach to women's rights issues (child care, family leave, reproductive choice) with a thin veneer of feminist rhetoric ("objectification of women").

Scapegoating pornography for misogyny, sex discrimination, or sexual violence in society not only threatens freedom of expression but does nothing to solve real world problems. As author Pat Califia writes,

> How can any intelligent woman believe that getting rid of pornography will make our lives better? If the American Family Association closed down every X-rated video store in the country, it wouldn't raise our wages, guarantee our reproductive rights, get rid of the idiotic images of women in advertising and the mass media, fund rape crisis centers and shelters for battered women, or promote AIDS education, cancer-screening programs, or prenatal care for women.[38]

Califia points out that while none of these health care and law enforcement programs gets adequate funding, our federal government spends millions trying to stamp out sexually arousing art and entertainment.

The MacKinnon-Dworkin antipornography campaign has also undermined the cause of women's rights. Obscenity laws have long been used to suppress information and art about female sexuality and reproduction. As author Robin Morgan points out, "a phallo-centric culture is more likely to begin its censorship purges with books on pelvic self-examination for women or books containing lyrical paeans to lesbianism than with *See Him Tear and Kill Her* or similar Mickey Spillanesque titles."[39] The original federal and state antiobscenity laws were specifically directed at birth control infor-mation, and these bans lasted well into the twentieth century.

This censorship of sex information in the supposed interests of protecting girls and women still goes on. In the last two decades, the classic, best-selling women's health care manual, *Our Bodies Ourselves* has been removed from school libraries in many localities. In 1980 *Our Bodies Ourselves* was banned by the Helena, Montana, school district; at one point during the controversy, the state prose-cutor threatened to bring criminal charges against any teacher who gave the book to a minor. In 1979 the Nashua, New Hampshire, school board removed *Ms.* magazine from the high school library because it contained classified ads for vibrators, contraceptives, and materials about lesbianism, witchcraft, trips to Cuba, and "commu-nist" folksingers. The novels of Judy Blume, which talk to and about adolescent girls and the sexual changes they experience, have been favorite targets of censorship in school and even public libraries.

An incident in late October 1992 dramatized the profoundly *anti*feminist nature of the MacKinnon-Dworkin censorship cam-paign. Law students at the University of Michigan invited a local artist, Carol Jacobsen, to mount an exhibit dealing with prostitu-tion to accompany a two-day academic conference on the subject. The conference was dominated by "protectionist" speakers who viewed prostitution as an evil to be eliminated. No working prosti-tute or representative of a prolegalization group was presented. One of the speakers complained that a videotape (by artist and former porn actress Veronica Vera) contained pornographic imagery and demanded that the students remove it. They did so, without consulting Jacobsen. When she discovered what had occurred, she protested, after which the entire exhibit was dismantled.

The Veronica Vera video, titled *Portrait of a Sexual Evolutionary*, is an autobiographical work that includes memories of a repressed Catholic girlhood, sexual awakening and experimentation, experiences in the porn industry, friendship with other women whom Vera describes as sexual adventurers or "shady Madonnas," and scenes of the filmmaker's congressional testimony in opposition to antipornography legislation. The work is by a woman, speaks to issues of women's liberation and sexuality, presents a libertarian political viewpoint—and was censored by people claiming to be feminists.

The impulse to stamp out pornography may always be with us—at least as long as the impulse to create and consume it lasts. Despite all the rhetoric and heated emotion surrounding the subject, censoring pornography is just another form of thought control. Suppressing sexual fantasies—or insisting on politically correct ones—is bad politics, bad feminism, and a bad idea.

✤ 8 ✤

Blasphemy, Subversiveness, and Other Sins

Blasphemy: *Profane or mocking speech, writing, or action concerning God or anything regarded as sacred.*

Sedition: *The stirring up of discontent, resistance, or rebellion against the government in power.*

—*Webster's New World Dictionary*

Sacred and Profane

N 1989 DONALD WILDMON'S AMERICAN FAMILY ASSO-ciation threatened Pepsi Cola with a boycott if the company didn't scrap plans for an ad campaign featuring the pop megastar and media genius Madonna. Wildmon's objection to Madonna was based on her "Like a Prayer" video. The video, like the song that inspired it, merges sexual and religious images in a manner familiar from centuries of classical art. The difference was that Madonna brought these themes up to date with an immediacy, and at a level of mass-marketing, that was a lot harder to ignore than masterpieces in museums.

In the same year, Wildmon, aided and abetted by Senator Jesse Helms and a host of others, attacked the artist Andres Serrano's photograph *Piss Christ*, entirely on the basis of the message they drew from its title. Serrano's work shows a crucifix immersed in shimmering fluid; it looks devotional, "virtually monumental as it floats, photographically enlarged, in a deep golden, rosy glow that is both ominous and glorious." The work would probably not have raised hackles "had the title not given away the process of its making."[1] It was irrelevant to the critics of *Piss Christ* that Serrano claimed he had not intended to offend; he did not view urine as repugnant. Combining the sacred symbol of the crucifix with something organic and human was a way of bringing God down to earth.

Serrano's intent in this sense wasn't so different from the Greek writer Nikos Kazantzakis in his novel *The Last Temptation of Christ*. And the same censorship impulse—to silence any artistic exploration of Christ's humanity—led to wild controversy in 1988 over the Martin Scorsese film made from Kazantzakis's best-selling book. This was probably the most virulent outbreak of religious hatred, deteriorating at times to violence, that America had seen in recent times.

In Los Angeles, fundamentalist preacher R. L. Hymers led angry crowds in demonstrations against *The Last Temptation of Christ*. They spray-painted and slashed movie screens, vandalized theaters, threatened to destroy all property of MCA, the parent company of the film's distributor, Universal, and publicly burned an effigy of Lew Wasserman, MCA's chairman.

Attacks on both MCA chairman Wasserman and the company's president, Sid Sheinberg, took on an ugly anti-Semitic tone. At one point, Reverend Hymers staged a demonstration featuring a mock crucifixion with a Christ figure screaming while a man portraying Wasserman nailed him to a ten-foot cross.[2] Three Republican congressmen contributed to the outbreak of sectarianism by introducing a legislative resolution that the film be withdrawn and all the distributor's businesses be boycotted. The Dallas, Texas, City Council passed a resolution condemning *Last Temptation*; Blockbuster Video announced that it would not carry the film; and both a community college and an entire county in Florida banned it.

The controversy had a mercenary edge. For $30, Reverend Jerry Falwell offered viewers of his Old Time Gospel Hour a "Last Temptation Battle Plan," complete with information packet and video on the life of Christ. Reverend Bill Bright, director of Campus Crusade for Christ, offered a $39.95 video on the same subject; while Wildmon's American Family Association sought tax-deductible contributions of $10 to $250 to finance its "Boycott MCA" campaign.[3]

Last Temptation portrayed Christ as a religiously inspired prophet but also as a human being resisting human desires, including the desire to experience marriage and sex. Director Scorsese wrote, "My film was made with deep religious feeling. . . . It is more than just another film project for me. I believe it is a religious film about suffering and the struggle to find God."[4]

Attacks on "blasphemous" art were a notable feature of the 1992 presidential campaign. In February of that year, Republican candidate Pat Buchanan aired a TV ad featuring clips from a documentary movie about gay black life called *Tongues Untied.* Superimposed over images of young black men dancing were the words "pornography," "blasphemy," and "too shocking to show." The message seemed to be that homosexuality (or perhaps interracial homosexuality) equaled blasphemy. Buchanan accused President Bush of spending taxpayers' money on this insult to traditional religion and morality.

Pat Buchanan's choice to attack George Bush for promoting blasphemy wasn't surprising, given the recent precedents—two years of escalating attacks on art and entertainment because of perceived offenses to Christianity. But the Buchanan affair—and Bush's response, the firing of NEA chair John Frohnmayer—are well worth pondering. It is an odd state of affairs when political leaders in the United States of America worry about being accused of religious heresies.

The idea behind the First Amendment was that everybody was to have freedom of speech, religion, and conscience. There was to be no religious orthodoxy, no governmental establishment of religion. We live in a secular, not a theocratic state. For the National Endowment for the Arts, or any government agency, to have imposed religious tests on applicants for arts grants would have been as improper and unconstitutional as a government ban on *Last Temptation*—or, in an earlier era, on Roberto Rossellini's film *The Miracle*—because their messages were perceived as "sacrilegious."

Such religious tests would also be unworkable. For one thing, whose religion would apply? And who from within any particular religious group would decide whether an ambiguous, multilayered work of art like *Piss Christ, Tongues Untied,* or *Last Temptation of Christ* was truly blasphemous?

The Supreme Court noted this anomaly in its 1952 decision condemning New York State's ban on *The Miracle* : "In seeking to apply the broad and all-inclusive definition of 'sacrilegious,'" the Court wrote, "the censor is set adrift upon a boundless sea amid a myriad of conflicting currents of religious views, with no charts but those provided by the most vocal and powerful orthodoxies."[5]

Political and Religious Orthodoxy: History and Current Reality

Even though the First Amendment prevents the government from prosecuting blasphemy in America today, the impulse that drives antiblasphemy crusades is powerful. History shows that people who are sure that their religion is the only path to salvation can be brutal and relentless in their efforts to silence all heresies. And when religious institutions become wealthy, powerful, and entrenched, they will act to maintain their power, much in the same way that governments traditionally do. Powerful churches, like governments, will often attack, demonize, isolate, vilify, and try to silence ideas that they perceive as threatening. It wasn't accidental that both the Catholic Church and the Protestant Film Office had powerful roles in American film censorship, as maintained by the industry's Hays Code until the 1960s.

It was precisely to prevent ideological control by powerful churches that the First Amendment to the U.S. Constitution mandated the separation of church and state. The First Amendment's "establishment clause" bars the government from imposing any religious orthodoxy or allying itself with any theological doctrine.

Some religious leaders view this as a sad state of affairs. Why, they ask, can sex education be taught in our public schools while a simple prayer is prohibited? But other religious leaders understand that separation of church and state is *not* an impediment, or a sign of hostility, to religion. On the contrary, separation is essential to individual freedom—the right to decide spiritual matters for ourselves—and to the freedom of religious institutions.

Once churches begin to entangle themselves with government, they're inevitably compromised. Sectarianism develops, with the favored church trying to promote its doctrines and suppress the others as heresies. So it was in Europe for centuries when popes reigned as secular rulers; so it was when the Church of England (established by Henry VIII so he could divorce his wife Catherine of Aragon and marry Anne Boleyn) went after Catholics and Puritans; and so it was in Puritan New England, where not only Christmas was outlawed but theater as well, on the ground that plays "increase immorality, impiety and contempt of religion."[6]

Art history is packed with instances of censorship caused by church disapproval of something it perceived as blasphemy. In the eighth century, the powerful leaders of the Catholic Church got together at the Second Council of Nicaea and came up with a long list of dos and don'ts for painting, being very specific when it came to what parts of the bodies of saints or other religious figures could be shown (the Virgin Mary could not be barefoot). Seven hundred years later, Church rules still dominated European art: at the 1563 Council of Trent the cardinals reiterated that painting and sculpture must strictly follow Catholic dogma. The church fathers understood that visual art was the "Bible of the illiterate"—a powerful storytelling tool to impress and indoctrinate the many people who could not read.

The Church was punctilious about even the greatest artists' adhering to the rules. The Inquisition interrogated the Renaissance artist Paolo Veronese after he painted a *Last Supper* that included dwarfs, jesters, servants, and a dog, all of which the inquisitors considered too vulgar and festive for so sanctified a subject. Veronese gamely defended his picture before the inquisitors in the name of artistic inspiration, and despite the intimidation made only minor changes. The Church seemed to be satisfied when Veronese shifted the title to the less sanctified *Feast in the House of Levi*.[7]

Artists throughout history have faced similar troubles. Caravaggio's *Death of the Virgin* altarpiece was rejected by the Church because the model was a prostitute. In the nineteenth century, Giuseppe Verdi's operas were regularly censored for both religious and political reasons. One work, *Stiffelio*, was so mutilated by censors' changes that the composer is believed to have destroyed the original score in despair, and never allowed the opera to be performed after its premiere. (The setting of another Verdi opera, *Un Ballo en Maschera*, had to be moved from eighteenth-century

Sweden to colonial Boston because the censors feared that the story, based on an actual assassination, would offend the Swedes.) In the twentieth century, the German artist George Grosz and his publisher were criminally prosecuted for blasphemy because of his bitterly satiric antiwar drawing, *Christ in a Gas Mask*.[8] One of the greatest novelists in history, Leo Tolstoy, was so depressed by pervasive government censorship that he wrote:

> You would not believe how, from the very commencement of my activity, that horrible censor question has tormented me. I wanted to write what I felt, but all the time it occurred to me that what I wrote would not be permitted, and involuntarily I had to abandon the work. I abandoned, and went on abandoning, and meanwhile the years passed away.[9]

Like blasphemy, supposedly subversive, politically dissenting, or seditious speech was censored and suppressed in England throughout most of its history. The United States also punished "seditious" words and thoughts during its early postcolonial years and, again, during and after World Wars I and II. The 1798 Sedition Act made it a crime to publish "false, scandalous and malicious" criticism of the government, and was aggressively used by the Federalist Party to silence and jail its Republican opponents. State sedition laws were used in the nineteenth century to punish and silence those who advocated the abolition of slavery. During World War I, new sedition laws banned any words reflecting "contempt or scorn" for the government.

The federal government used these laws to censor art. During World War I, the U.S. Post Office revoked the mailing privileges of scores of periodicals because of perceived disloyalty to the war effort. The most famous was probably *The Masses*, a radical, antiwar journal that featured brilliant, incisive political cartoons.

The government claimed that much of the material in *The Masses* violated the federal Espionage Act, which empowered the Post Office to withhold from the mail any material promoting "treason, insurrection or forcible resistance to any law of the United States."

The artworks for which *The Masses* was censored included two cartoons by the artist Henry Glitenkamp, one, titled "Conscription," showing a crumbling Liberty Bell, and the other depicting a cannon with nude men labeled "Youth" and "Labor" chained to it; another satiric cartoon, by Boardman Robinson, entitled "Making the World Safe for Capitalism"; a drawing by artist Art Young showing arms manufacturers shooing away Congress and saying, "Run along now! We got through with you when you declared war for us!"; and articles and a poem defending the rights of conscientious objectors.[10]

When *The Masses* challenged the Post Office decision as a violation of its First Amendment rights, federal judge Learned Hand ruled in the magazine's favor. Hand said that political protest, even in wartime, was part of free speech, and shouldn't be equated with "direct incitement to violent resistance." But Judge Hand was promptly overruled by a federal appeals court. *The Masses* went out of business, its editors were criminally prosecuted, and Hand's view of the First Amendment as protecting all "seditious" speech except actual incitement to violence was forgotten for the time being.

It wasn't till the sixties that the Supreme Court put a stop to the business of punishing politically dissenting or subversive speech. The main purpose of the First Amendment, the Court finally recognized, was to get rid of the laws against "seditious libel" that were so popular with English kings, and to permit the "uninhibited, robust, and wide-open" political debate essential to democracy. Under our system of freedom, even violently unpatriotic or anarchistic rhetoric cannot be silenced or punished unless it's actually intended, and likely, to incite imminent lawless conduct. Incendiary exhortations to an already riled-up crowd might meet this standard; but it's unlikely that a book, an article, a play, or a song, ever could.[11]

There are at least three important reasons for this rule of constitutional law. First, short of real, direct incitement, we just don't want to give government the power to decide what kind of radical, angry, incendiary, even revolutionary speeches, songs, paintings, or books should be suppressed. Unless real, direct incitement to imminent harm can be shown, even fiery outbursts of political rhetoric are an important part of our political dialogue. And since all governments seek to maintain power and suppress criticism, they're likely to exaggerate the harm created by any challenge to their credibility or rhetorical threat to the status quo.

Second, in a free society, we have the right to criticize, and hear our fellow citizens criticize, the government at all levels. Such criticism needn't be and often isn't polite. Angry raps about police abuse in minority communities, even raps expressing a thirst for revenge against perceived injustices, revolutionary exhortations to overthrow capitalism, bitterly satiric speeches, editorials, and cartoons savaging political figures—all must be protected. Uninhibited debate on public issues—hence, change and reform—can only happen if political dissent of all emotional temperatures is allowed to be heard.

Third is the "pressure-cooker" theory of free expression. Radical, antiestablishment, even violent speech, is an important safety valve. It gives people a way to let off steam. Violent revolution is ultimately less likely when dissent is allowed to flourish and churn up the forces necessary for peaceful change. As one critic of the extraordinary furor that surrounded an incendiary rock 'n' roll song in 1992 observed, "I'd rather see these kids release their frustrations [through music] than express their anger in some other way."[12]

The Prophets of Rap and the Tranquillity of the State

In July 1992 famed Iran-Contra conspirator Oliver North jumped on a rapidly accelerating political bandwagon of prominent officials and police associations. The cause against which all the verbal fire-power was amassed was a musician, Ice-T, his producer, Time Warner, and his heavy-metal rock song, "Cop Killer." The song appeared on an album called *Body Count*, whose unifying theme was racism in all its guises, from the Ku Klux Klan to blacks who believe that all whites are "no good." Exaggerated acts of violence were described as the album progressed; the *Cop Killer* cut at the end was a heated, angry, coarse, rude, fiery, and frightening rap about one man's quest for revenge against police brutality. *Body Count* was only one example of a growing musical culture that expressed the aggressively angry feelings of some African American youths in powerful metaphors of violence and revenge.

According to North—as well as the National Rifle Association, the attorney general of California, Vice President Dan Quayle, and numerous police and sheriffs' associations around the country—"Cop Killer" was an unambiguous call to kill police officers and should promptly be withdrawn from circulation. Moreover, said North, Ice-T and Time Warner should be prosecuted under sedition and anarchy laws. Police and prosecutors pressured music stores to stop selling the album, and police associations threatened boycotts of all Time Warner products until their demands were met.

Ice-T defended the song, describing it as the angry fictional monologue of a black victim of police brutality—not a call to violence but a dramatization of the emotions and mindset of the victim. (The narrator sings, "I'm 'bout to kill me somethin'/ A pig stopped me for nuthin'!") Time Warner's president, Gerald Levin, wrote an eloquent defense both of the music's message and of the musician's right to sing it. The song, said Levin, was about "race and poverty and violence and frustration."

> It doesn't incite or glorify violence. It's a song about how one of those kids reacts in the wake of the well-known—and not so well-known—incidents in which a small number of police have used excessive force. One-sided, violent, and scatological, it's the artist's rap on how a person in the street feels. It's his fictional-ized attempt to get inside a character's head. It's a shout of pain and protest and in this it shares a long history with rock and older forms of urban music. "Cop Killer" is no more a call for gunning down police than "Frankie and Johnny" is a summons for jilted lovers to shoot one another.[13]

To acquiesce in demands that Time Warner withdraw the album, said Levin, would "be a destructive precedent. It would be a signal to all the artists and journalists inside and outside Time Warner that if they wish to be heard, then they must tailor their minds and souls to fit the reigning orthodoxies."

Neither Levin's nor Ice-T's explanations calmed the waters. They certainly didn't make the critics any less eager to suppress the message that they heard in the music. That message, as Ice-T's defenders pointed out, was police abuse. And despite the police associations' angry rhetoric, it was a message that needed to be heard.

The problem of police abuse is invisible to many Americans, but it is an all-too-visible and urgent problem for those who live in our mostly-minority inner-city neighborhoods. Many Americans may never have experienced physical or verbal abuse by a police officer. Few residents of the inner cities *haven't* had the experience, or at least known somebody who has. Racist invective, gratuitous brutality, demeaning strip searches, unjustified arrests, and the "code of silence" that compels most police officers—even those (the great majority) who are not abusive themselves—not to "blow the whistle" on their comrades, all combine to make many poor people, particularly minority youths, feel angry and victimized. Given the fear and humiliation that police abuse engenders, the incendiary rage and macho posturing of Ice-T in "Cop Killer" (and many other rap and rock artists) is understandable. That may be why a number of minority police officers' associations, understanding the rage, opposed efforts to suppress the album.

Oliver North and his cohorts didn't find a prosecutor to charge Ice-T or Time Warner with sedition, but they succeeded nonetheless in getting the song suppressed. Several weeks after the controversy began, and after rumors began circulating that the company was looking for a way out of a media-fed frenzy that just wouldn't go away, Ice-T himself announced that he would withdraw the song because of death threats that Time Warner employees had been receiving. The company insisted it didn't pressure the artist, but it certainly seemed relieved.

The source of the death threats against Time Warner may never be known, but the irony of some of the police association pressure tactics was inescapable. Gerald Arenberg, executive director of the National Association of Chiefs of Police, was quoted during the "Cop Killer" controversy as saying that police "could create a living hell for all of Time Warner's cable systems" by, for example, giving the company's repair trucks parking tickets.[14] Yet, as Arenberg surely knew, singling out any citizen for specially harsh treatment because of that citizen's music, books, films, or other artistic expression is unconstitutional: it's punishment for exercising free speech. Unlike

Ice-T's angry metaphors, this was a genuine threat of unlawful conduct, with the force of government authority behind it.

The outcome of the "Cop Killer" crusade was unfortunate. Not
only was this song withdrawn, but Time Warner and other producers became newly edgy and self-censorious about other music
with problematic lyrics. Yet protest music is one of the few outlets
for expression of political outrage that's available to people without
a lot of power. The suppression of "Cop Killer," as one critic
observed, added "a new mechanism" to the repertory of censorship:
"if police groups don't like a song, they can make it disappear."[15]

The attack on Ice-T and Time Warner was probably the first
time, in the several years of ideological warfare between law
enforcement groups and rap musicians, that anyone had invoked
sedition laws. But North's idea was perhaps inevitable. If obscenity
can be punished, if blasphemy is a basis for denying government
grants or benefits, why not sedition as a reason for censoring
unpalatable music? Especially if that music, with its violent
metaphors and macho rhetoric, is reminiscent of the Black Panther
and Black Muslim politics of an earlier generation:

> Rap is intense and can be very frightening to outsiders. Political
> rap groups like Public Enemy and Professor Griff are as intimi-
> dating as the Black Panthers or the Black Muslims were in their
> time. But what is being expressed is what is being said, thought
> and felt within those hard-street communities.[16]

Before the Ice-T episode, the major musical targets of law
enforcement anger were rap groups like Public Enemy and N.W.A.,
and especially N.W.A.'s leader, Ice Cube. In 1989, the N.W.A.
album *Straight Outta Compton*, with its unambiguous song "Fuck
Tha' Police," inspired the FBI's assistant director of public affairs,
Milt Ahlerich, to write a letter to the group's distributors "taking

exception" to the work because it "encourages violence against and disrespect for the law enforcement officer." Claiming that the music was "discouraging and degrading" to police, Ahlerich added, "I wanted you to be aware of the FBI's position relative to this song and its message. I believe my views reflect the opinion of the entire law enforcement community." The ACLU's Barry Lynn called the letter "censorship by intimidation": "He's clearly trying to characterize this as an official position of the FBI, and that's what takes it beyond the scope of just the opinion of an elected official."[17]

Private police associations undoubtedly have a First Amendment right to protest rap music and even to demand its removal from the marketplace. When police start acting in their official government capacities, though, the picture changes. The FBI's letter to distributors, like the Meese Commission's 1986 letter to retail store chains that carried *Playboy*, *Penthouse*, and the like (see Chapter 3), crossed the line from simple expressions of opinion to government actions with an unambiguous censorship purpose.

Flag Art

Art that uses the powerful symbol of the American flag has often created an emotional furor fully equal to the attack on rap musicians. Some veterans groups have on occasion reacted with genuine frenzy to an artist or museum displaying a work with a flag on the floor, or incorporated into the imagery in a less than reverent way. Yet what could be more traditionally American, and closer to the core purposes of the First Amendment (to protect and promote political debate) than art that uses the powerful symbol of the flag to make statements of protest, anger, bitterness, irony, or disillusion?

"Disrespectful" artistic uses of the American flag date at least to the early 1960s, when a New York City art gallery was invaded by police who had received reports that the exhibit on display included a flag-wrapped phallic symbol and another flag in the shape of a human body hanging from a noose. Both works were intended as protests of the Vietnam War. The gallery owner was criminally charged and convicted under New York's flag desecration law. Eventually a federal court ruled that the conviction was invalid because the sculptures were protected by the First Amendment.

The musical *Hair* was also censored in part because of its use of "flag art." In one scene, a member of the cast is wrapped in an American flag. Public officials in Atlanta, Georgia, refused permission for *Hair* to be staged at the city's civic center, in part because, they said, the scene would violate the state's flag desecration law. A federal court ordered Atlanta to allow *Hair* to proceed.

It wasn't until the late 1980s that the Supreme Court made plain that the First Amendment prohibited punishing people for burning or otherwise desecrating an American flag. The highly provocative nature of the act only reinforced the point that it was symbolic speech—an expression of political protest. Yet controversy and censorship continued to follow not only flag-burning but flag art.

In 1989 in Chicago a student work called *What is the Proper Way to Display a U.S. Flag?* prompted the city to enact an ordinance entitled "Desecration of Flags," banning virtually any use of the symbol. Nine artists sued to challenge the law, and a state court judge, following Supreme Court precedents, struck it down.

Three years later, the same work was shown at the Visual Art Center in Anchorage, Alaska. Members of a local veterans group stole the original flag, then persisted in removing every substitute that the center bought to replace it. Finally, the charade ended when it became clear that the center had a large supply of cheap replacement flags.

In 1992 a sculpture by Oklahoma artist Rick Freeman entitled "Home of the Homeless, Amen" was pulled from a local art exhibit and hidden in a broom closet after complaints from local veterans and others. The sculpture consisted of a shopping cart on top of an American flag; inside the cart was a pair of praying hands. The work, evidently a commentary on the gap between the promise of American prosperity and the reality of poverty, had won a prize in the town's annual art exhibition. The art gallery, trying to justify its action, cited a long-moribund federal law commanding respect for the flag.

Retaliation for discomfiting political messages took on a new twist in Frederick County, Maryland, in 1991, when legislators refused to submit a bill that would have provided support for a local arts center after the center had displayed a political painting opposing the Persian Gulf War and satirizing President Bush, Senator Jesse Helms, General Norman Schwarzkopf, and others. This work didn't have any flags, but, among other improprieties, it showed Bush nude from the waist down. (Helms had a Roman breastplate and no pants.) The lawmakers who were so offended by this artistic irreverence obviously forgot folk poet Bob Dylan's warning that "even the President of the United States sometimes must have to stand naked."

Flag art, incendiary political raps, "blasphemous" images, all face threats of censorship by government officials and private groups. Because the First Amendment so clearly protects these provocative forms of expression, the censorship usually comes in subtler forms than criminal prosecution.

One such form is pressure brought to bear on distributors and retailers. Surely, those angered by the messages of rap music or flag art have a right to protest, to raise questions, to talk about the issues. And the musicians have a right to respond. Protest and pressure have in some instances contributed to modulating irresponsible or poisonous messages—for example, the anti-Semitism in Public Enemy's early recordings. But when the pressure is not for "more speech" but less, for suppression of music because of dangers perceived in the ideas it expresses, one of the very purposes of the First Amendment—to get angry ideas out in the open—is frustrated. The Oliver Norths of the world *can* do society a service by raising the issue, but not if they try to win the debate by silencing their opponents.

The other major way that censorship of allegedly seditious, blasphemous, or otherwise offensive speech occurs is in the manipulation of government programs. Not only are agencies like the NEA and the NEH (National Endowment for the Humanities) under pressure to apply political and religious litmus tests in their grant-making, but government benefits that should be available to all, like access to public exhibition spaces, are increasingly being parceled out on ideological grounds. California artist Dayton Claudio, whose prochoice painting *Sex, Laws, and Coathangers* was unceremoniously ousted from a Raleigh, North Carolina, federal building in 1992, despite his possession of a permit for its exhibition, is just one example. (The building manager claimed the work was "obscene, controversial, and political.")

The epidemic of book-banning that has overtaken our public schools in recent years is another manifestation of mounting pressures to censor allegedly seditious or blasphemous art and literature. School boards throughout the country have responded to pressures, usually from small groups of fundamentalist parents, to remove works not only because of profane language, but because their subject is unacceptable to someone's idea of religious orthodoxy. Books about "the occult," from simple collections of Halloween tricks to studies of cultural traditions like voodoo, have been purged from school library shelves. Said one Arizona parent who protested a book of Halloween stories, "Children are drawn in to want more. Before you know it, your adolescent is caught up in Satanism."[18]

A Florida school superintendent in 1987 had another justification for his removal of hundreds of books from school classrooms. Reading, he explained, "is where you get ideas from. It puts ideas into their [the students'] heads."[19]

The agenda of many of these groups may be less to remove material that they think is blasphemous than to argue for "equal time," so that they can insert their particular religious doctrine into classrooms. Lawsuits have been brought, for example, to remove a reading series called *Impressions* from public schools on the theory that it promotes the "religion" of witchcraft and the occult. Benjamin Bull, lead attorney for Donald Wildmon's American Family Association and lawyer for the parents in a California case, explained that "if witchcraft and neo-paganism are religions—and we know they are—then children cannot be allowed to role-play the practices and employ the tenets of those religions if they cannot do the same for Christianity."[20]

Censorship of art and literature because of blasphemy or subversiveness has a long, dense history that, obviously, is still with us. Artists have always run afoul of attempts to censor irreverent and confrontational speech, and they always will. Artists will continue to use powerful religious and political symbols in ways deemed disrespectful by church or government authorities. Exploring and defining—and sometimes questioning and mocking—the reigning orthodoxies has always been a function of art.

In 1991, a remarkable art exhibit toured America. Titled *Entartete Kunst,* or "Degenerate Art," it documented Nazi Germany's attacks in the thirties on art, literature, and music that was considered unpatriotic, blasphemous, confusing, decadent, Jewish-influenced, or otherwise insufficiently Aryan and supportive of National Socialist ideology. Virtually all modern nontraditional art works were removed by the truckload from German museums and collected in the huge "Degenerate Art" show in Munich. Many works were affixed with a red sticker stating, "Paid for by the taxes of the German working people."[21]

Although we need to be careful about making facile comparisons to other nations and other times, there's no question that the rhetoric used in the censorship wars during the eighties and nineties bears uncanny resemblance to the way that the Nazi regime in Germany demonized unconventional groups and manipulated human emotions. The 1991 "Degenerate Art" show provided a vivid reminder that before the Nazis mocked, segregated, disenfranchised, and then destroyed Jews, radicals, and homosexuals, they mocked, segregated, banned, and burned allegedly "degenerate" Jewish, modernist, sexually suspect, or socialist literature and art. And in doing so, they pushed many of the same hot buttons—particularly blasphemy and the waste of taxpayers' money—that are used in today's censorship wars.

Censorious impulses and strains of intolerance are still with us and surface when demagogues succeed in demonizing artists for supposedly subversive, "degenerate," or blasphemous creations.

❧ CONCLUSION ❧

Scapegoating Speech

Censorship can't eliminate evil; it can only kill freedom.

—Garrison Keillor[1]

WHETHER WE'RE TALKING ABOUT DISCOMFORTING RELIgious imagery, frank sex, simple nudity, "occultism" in music, irreverent use of flag symbols, or other forms of dissent, censors perennially blame artistic expression for the ills of society. Overliteral readings of complex works, and mechanistic thinking about the relation between images, ideas, and acts, drive many campaigns to suppress music, movies, books, theater, and visual art.

But words and images don't cause bad acts. Messages in art are influenced by social conditions and attitudes, not the other way around. In the words of a Texas rock musician, "There's nothing more obscene than reality. The world is more terrifying than anything *we* could ever say about it."[2]

We humans are complicated creatures who can rarely point to any one factor, whether hereditary or environmental, as determining our character and behavior. The reasons for our social ills lie in the real world, not in the world of imagination. A theater critic put it very well: "I do not believe," he wrote in 1992, "that role models in pop culture determine what kind of adults children will become; if that were the case, my entire generation would resemble Lucy and Ricky Ricardo."[3]

Scapegoating speech is a dangerous excuse for refusing to deal with real-world problems. It sacrifices the thing that is most unique and precious about the United States—freedom of speech—in pursuit of an elusive and falsely oversimplified solution to social ills, and it distracts us from searching for real solutions. One can only wonder why some political leaders prefer these distractions—prefer to invent and attack demons and scapegoats instead of seriously addressing the tough, massive problems of poverty, homelessness, a stagnating economy, crushing debt, destructive racial divisions, widening economic disparities, and the heavy burdens borne by poor and single women, to name a few.

A 1992 article about Iran suggests that politicians' reasons for scapegoating speech may be universal. The reporter noted that accusations of blasphemy against Salman Rushdie's novel *The Satanic Verses* raised a furor in Muslim countries that "emboldened the mullahs to use it as a diversion from frustration and malaise at home."[4] In Iran as elsewhere, focusing on hot-button symbolic issues like religion, patriotism, sex, or "family values" is a convenient distraction from worsening social conditions. At least, history suggests that witchhunts against unpopular, dissident, or minority groups and views often emerge at such traumatic moments.

Blaming words or images is not merely an ineffective way to address social problems; it ignores both the cathartic and consciousness-raising functions of art. If feelings of anger, frustration, protest, or desperation can be expressed through the creative process, they're less likely to explode in antisocial behavior. And if society can see itself through the mirror of art, it will be more likely to pay attention to social ills than if unfortunate ideas or realities are suppressed and ignored.

A Spin Doctor for Free Speech

Is there no limit, then, to freedom of speech? (This is a question ACLU attorneys are often asked.) Does the First Amendment mean that, in the words of the classic Cole Porter song, "Anything Goes"?

Not quite. There are exceptions to the sweeping language of the First Amendment ("Congress shall make *no law* . . . abridging the freedom of speech. . . ."). But those exceptions for the most part are narrow, and properly so. Actual incitement to imminent violence, false advertising, extortion, threats—these forms of speech may be prohibited because they directly cause serious harm to identifiable individuals.

Artistic expression almost never fits within one of the narrow First Amendment exceptions. And again, properly so. The dangers of giving government the power to censor art—even bad or offensive art—are too great. Letting the government suppress ideas and images that it decides are provocative, nasty, repugnant, or just plain wrong is a "cure" for bad speech that's worse than the disease.

These simple principles are so often forgotten. In every aspect of the censorship struggle, we see highly emotional attacks on ideas and images found in music, movies, books, and visual art. The attackers may be sincere, or they may simply be hypocrites trying to raise money or attract votes by manipulating many Americans' deeply held beliefs and fears about sex, religion, and patriotism. But in either case, defending free speech under these circumstances can be a daunting task.

You can't always reason with powerful, highly charged images. A picture of a naked woman in chains, a highly graphic homosexual act, an artist stepping on an American flag, or a crucifix in urine, can, depending on the audience, stop all reasoned discourse. Ideas like free speech, diversity, and tolerance often can't compete on an emotional level.

Maybe the First Amendment needs a spin doctor. It is not always an easy product to sell. Most Americans agree with the principle of free expression, but rebel when it comes to words and ideas we find heinous or hateful.

That's natural. We tend to like free speech in the abstract, and of course want our own rights protected, but remarkably large numbers of us consistently tell pollsters that the line should be drawn at whatever type of speech we find particularly threatening or offensive.

A good spin doctor would bring to life the values of tolerance and diversity—values like allowing people (including artists and pop singers) to sound off about their anger, to reflect the rage of their communities or the troubling urges that are part of being human.

This ideal press agent would dramatize the dangers of allowing government—whether city, state, or national—to decide what's a good message and what's a bad one. He or she would dramatize one of the most insidious results of censorship: blacklisting and witch-hunts. With the "communist menace" having disappeared, America is in grave danger of finding new demons among any group that challenges the imagined "traditional values" utopia of our mythical past: sexual nonconformists, provocative artists, pornographers, flag burners, or other political dissidents.

America has been down this road before. Whether it was women accused of witchcraft in colonial Salem, Massachusetts, or radicals and idealists accused of subversion after Worlds Wars I and II, demonizing people who have threatening ideas starts a ritual of hysterical "purification" that can be hard to stop, and that endangers everyone's liberty. Our spin doctor would persuade us to beware of demagogues who create demons for us to scapegoat and hate, be they artists, gays, uppity women, posturing revolutionaries, TV characters, or "East Coast boutique liberals."

Finally, our spin doctor would demonstrate that scapegoating speech is a dangerous excuse for refusing to deal with real-world problems—that some of the art and entertainment targeted for censorship these days may even have real value. We may sometimes need to hear messages that are harsh and unpleasant. And, finally, that arts censorship is a bad idea because artists are our muses and prophets. They speak to us of nightmares but also of dreams. They rage against cruelty and inhumanity but also celebrate the sweetness of life.

AFTERWORD

〰〰〰〰〰〰〰〰〰〰〰〰〰〰〰〰〰〰〰〰〰〰〰〰〰〰〰〰〰〰

What You Can Do

If you are persuaded that scapegoating speech is a bad idea, here are some of the things you can do:

- Help organize an anticensorship group in your community. The procensorship folks are already very well organized. Freedom can't be preserved if the people who care about it do nothing until there's an immediate crisis. When there isn't such a crisis brewing, you can get ready by forming networks with librarians, students, teachers, writers and other artists, like-minded parents and kids, managers of book, music, and video stores, and assorted other civil libertarians. Hold educational events about the history and current dangers of censorship.

- Write letters, send telegrams, make phone calls to your legislators and other public officials, and do it often. Tell them you object to your tax money being wasted in efforts to prosecute musicians, other artists, or producers of sexually explicit works. Tell them you oppose content restrictions on arts funding, and want to see the NEA fulfill its original purpose—encouraging artistic freedom and innovation. Tell them how much you care about the issue and don't forget to remind them that you and your friends and family vote.

- Write editorials and letters to the editor making the same point. Talk to arts and law reporters in your local media about the anticensorship point of view.

- Get involved in political campaigns. Support candidates who recognize that crackdowns on pornography, rock music, the NEA, and "blasphemous" art, are cynical distractions from the real problems we face as a society. Oppose candidates who engage in demagoguery on these issues. Educate the wafflers and make them take a position.

- Follow Justice Louis Brandeis's advice that the remedy for bad messages in art or politics is "more speech, not enforced silence."[1] More speech could mean, for example, addressing the racism and misogyny that we hear in some rap music (and in other arts), as well as encouraging and giving fair commercial breaks to female artists and others who may have more egalitarian messages. More speech could mean taking the lessons of some pornography research to heart and devising educational and public relations programs to combat rape myths and other hypermasculinity propaganda that distorts the psychosexual lives of both men and women.

- Point to real solutions to real problems when the prodecency squads start scapegoating speech. If politically inflammatory rap music is the target, point out some things that could be done to relieve police-minority tensions in inner cities. If it's too much casual sex on TV, propose ways to talk about the issue and educate kids about responsible sexual behavior.

NOTES

Acknowledgments

1. Words spoken by the late Congressman Ted Weiss to the House Subcommittee on Postsecondary Education, April 4, 1990; quoted in Richard Bolton, ed., *Culture Wars* (The New Press, 1992), p. 166.

Introduction to the Revised Edition

1. *Reno v. ACLU*, 117 S. Ct. 2329, 2351, 2344, 2340, (1997) (quoting in part the findings and opinions of the three lower court judges who originally heard the case: *ACLU v Reno*, 929 F.Supp.824, 883 (E.D.Pa. 1996) (Dalzell, J.); ibid. at 842).

2. For more on the frailties of rating and blocking programs, see Marjorie Heins, "Screening Out Sex," *The American Prospect*, July-August 1998, p. 38.

3. See generally Marjorie Heins, *Indecency: The Ongoing American Debate Over Sex, Children, Free Speech, and Dirty Words*, Andy Warhol Foundation for the Visual Arts Paper Series on the Arts, Culture, and Society, No. 7 (1997).

4. *Tinker v. Des Moines Independent School District*, 393 U.S. 503, 506, 511 (1969).

5. *Board of Education v. Pico*, 457 U.S. 853, 857 (1982).

6. Ibid. at 868-69 (internal quotations omitted).

7. Ibid. at 870-71.

8. *Bethel School District v. Fraser*, 478 U.S. 675 (1986); *Hazelwood School District v. Kuhlmeier*, 484 U.S. 260 (1988).

9. *Lacks v. Ferguson Reorganized School District*, 147 F.3d 718, 1998 U.S.App. LEXIS 13187, *17 (8th Cir. 1998).

10. *Boring v. Buncombe County Board of Education*, 136 F.3d 364, 370 (4th Cir. 1998), quoting Plato, *The Republic: Book II* (Jowett trans., Walter J. Black, Inc. 1942), p. 281.

11. Personal Responsibility and Work Opportunity Reconciliation Act of 1996, P. L. 104-193, 104th Congress, 42 U.S.C.§ 710 (1996).

12. See, e.g., Alan Guttmacher Institute, *Sex and America's Teenagers* (The Alan Guttmacher Institute, 1994); National Research Council, *Risking the Future: Adoles-*

cent Sexuality, Pregnancy and Child-bearing (National Academy Press, 1987); Jeff Stryker, "Abstinence or else," *The Nation,* June 16, 1997, p.19.

13. See *Finley v. National Endowment for the Arts,* 100 F.3d 671, 681-83 (9th Cir. 1996), reversed, 118 S.Ct 2168 (1998).

14. *National Endowment for the Arts v. Finley,* 118 S.Ct. at–, 66 U.S.L.W. at 4591.

15. Ibid.

16. The three were Antonin Scalia, Clarence Thomas, and David Souter. In addition to stating that the "decency and respect" standard was viewpoint-based, all three of these justices agreed that the majority's reading of the law to be only advisory was not credible, because Congress's message to the NEA had been clear–disfavor indecent or disrespectful art. Scalia and Thomas would have ruled that such mandated viewpoint discrimination was perfectly acceptable in a government funding program, and chided the majority angrily for "sustaining the constitutionality" of the law "by gutting it." Ibid. at 4591. Only Justice Souter agreed with the plaintiffs that the law was unconstitutional because unlike funding programs where the government is paying to deliver its own message or buying art to decorate its own property, the NEA was created to support "freedom of thought, imagination, and inquiry." Ibid. at 4598.

17. Frank Rich, "Thin-Skinned U.S.A.," *The New York Times,* June 26, 1998, p. A15.

Introduction

1. Susan Sontag, quoted in *The New York Times Magazine,* August 2, 1992, p. 43.

2. *Cohen v. California,* 403 U.S. 15, 25 (1971).

3. *Winters v. New York,* 333 U.S. 507, 510 (1948).

4. *Planned Parenthood of Southern Pennsylvania v. Casey,* 505 U.S.833, 851 (1992).

5. *Zamora v. Columbia Broadcasting System,* 480 F.Supp. 199, 206 (S.D. Fla. 1979).

6. *Olivia N. v. National Broadcasting Company,* 126 Cal.App.3d 488, 495 (1981). The Brandeis quote is from *Whitney v. California,* 274 U.S. 357 (1927), an early "sedition" case (see Chapter 8).

7. John Leland, "Rock and Roll Under Siege," *New York Newsday,* Aug. 27, 1990, p. 5.

8. *Waller v. Ozzy Osbourne,* 763 F.Supp. 1144, 1150, 1151 (M.D. Ga. 1991), affirmed in unpublished opinion (11th Cir., Mar. 2, 1992), cert. denied, 506 U.S. 916 (1992).

Heads?) Roll," *New York Times*,
Nov. 2, 1992, p. C13.

10. Janet Maslin, "Sexual Obses-
sion, Edited for an R," *New York
Times*, Dec. 23, 1992, p. C13.

Chapter 3

1. *Bantam Books* v. *Sullivan*, 372
U.S. 58, 68 (1963).

2. *Bantam Books* v. *Sullivan*, 372
U.S. at 68.

3. *Penthouse International, Ltd.* v.
Meese, 939 F.2d 1011, 1015 (D.C. Cir. 1991),
cert. denied, 117 L.Ed.2d 650 (1992).

4. *Skyywalker Records, Inc.* v. *Navarro*, 739 F.Supp. 578, 598 (S.D. Fla.
1990), reversed in part on the issue
of obscenity, 960 F.2d 134 (11th Cir.),
cert. denied, 61 U.S.L.W. 3418
(Dec.7, 1992).

Chapter 4

1. *Skyywalker Records, Inc.* v. *Navarro*, 739 F.Supp. 578, 594 (S.D.
Fla. 1990), reversed, 960 F.2d 134
(11th Cir.), cert. denied, 61 U.S.L.W.
3418 (Dec. 7, 1992).

2. *Skyywalker Records*, 739 F.Supp.
at 596.

3. *Luke Records, Inc.* v. *Navarro*, 960
F.2d 134, 135 (11th Cir. 1992), cert.
denied, 61 U.S.L.W. 3418 (Dec. 7, 1992).

4. Quoted in David Szatmary,
*Rockin' in Time: A Social History of Rock
and Roll* (Prentice Hall, 1991), p. 25.

5. Ibid., p. 24.

6. Ibid., pp. 25, 53.

7. Incidents recounted in ibid.,
pp. 50, 96, 131–32.

8. Ibid., pp. 232–33.

9. Ibid., p. 184.

10. Ibid., p. 193.

11. Irvin Molotsky, "Hearings on
Rock Lyrics," *New York Times*, Sept.
20, 1985, p. 8.

12. "Tipper Gore Widens War on
Rock," *New York Times*, Jan. 4, 1988,
p. C18.

13. See Joan Delfattore, *What
Johnny Shouldn't Read: Textbook
Censorship in America* (Yale Univer-
sity Press, 1992), p. 146.

14. For a handsome coffee table
compilation of torture and sadism in
classical art, see Lionelli Puppi, *Tor-
ment in Art: Pain, Violence, and Martyrdom* (Rizzoli, 1991).

15. Clay McNear, "It's Only
Rock 'n' Roll," *Dallas Observer*, Sept.
12, 1985.

16. Steven Lee Myers, "When the
Law and Music Clash, Uproar Fol-
lows," *New York Times*, Jan. 10, 1992,
p. B1.

17. Jon Pareles, "Debate Spurs
Hearings on Rating Rock Lyrics,"
New York Times, Sept. 18, 1985, p. 21.

18. Charles Krauthammer, "X
Ratings for Rock?" *Washington Post*,
Sept. 20, 1985, p. A27.

Chapter 5

1. Kenneth Clark, *The Nude* (Princeton University Press, 1956), p. 27.

2. Anne-Imelda Radice, Acting Chair of the National Endowment for the Arts, Testimony to the U.S. House of Representatives Committee on Appropriations, May 5, 1992.

3. *Barnes* v. *Glen Theatre, Inc.*, 115 L.Ed. 2d 504, 514 (1991).

4. Gillian Hanson, *Original Skin: Nudity and Sex in Cinema and Theatre* (Tom Stacey, Ltd., 1970), p. 165, quoting Rosemary Shevlin, *New York Times*, June 22, 1969.

5. Lee Mishkin, "Hair Explodes on Broadway," *Morning Telegraph*, May 1, 1968.

6. Jack Kroll, "Eros Goes Public," *Newsweek*, June 30, 1969, p. 81.

7. Hanson, *Original Skin*, p. 165.

8. Clark, *The Nude*, pp. 309–10.

9. Ibid., p. 3.

10. Jane Clapp describes these incidents in *Art Censorship: A Chronology of Proscribed and Prescribed Art* (Scarecrow Press, 1972), pp. 93, 97, 107, 110.

11. Ibid., p. 145.

12. Ibid., p. 240.

13. Havelock Ellis, the British reformer and champion of sexual freedom, in his 1922 *On Life and Sex* (Mentor ed., 1957), p. 183.

14. Tony Brown and Rob Urban, "Nudity Scene Altered," *Charlotte Observer*, Dec. 8, 1990, p. 4B.

15. Peter Goodman, "Schoenberg's Moses," *New York Newsday*, Sept. 16, 1990, sec. 2, p. 27.

16. Octavio Roca, "Irresistible Ewing Gives Life to Fine 'Salome,'" *Washington Times*, Nov. 5, 1990, p. E1.

17. Tim Page, "A Salome Brimming with Mania," *New York Newsday*, Nov. 6, 1990, pt.1, p. 2.

18. In the opinion of, among others, *New York Times* photography critic Andy Grundberg (*Camera*, June 3, 1990), p. 67.

19. See also Stephen Dubin's *Arresting Images: Impolitic Art and Uncivil Actions* (Routledge, 1992), pp. 170–90.

20. On the genesis and power of "sex panics," see Carole S. Vance's articles, "Reagan's Revenge: Restructuring the NEA," *Art in America*, Nov. 1990, p. 49; and "The War on Culture," *Art in America*, Sept. 1989, p. 39.

21. Sibella Connor, "Figuratively Speaking," *Richmond Times-Dispatch*, Nov. 8, 1992, p. 11.

22. Both Florida incidents are recounted in the American Library Association's *Newsletter on Intellectual Freedom*, Sept. 1991, p. 161.

23. "Album Cover Change," *New York Times*, Aug. 21, 1991, p. C12.

24. Nat Hentoff, "Francisco Jose de Goya Convicted of Sexual Harassment," *Village Voice*, Jan. 14, 1992; author's interview with university public relations officer, Dec. 8, 1992.

25. These instances are recounted in Clapp, *Art Censorship*, pp. 323, 325.

26. Robert Atkins, "Scene & Heard," *Village Voice*, Dec. 10, 1991, p. 102; National Coalition Against Censorship, *Censorship News*, No. 3, Issue 40, 1991.

Chapter 6

1. Preamble to the National Endowment for the Arts and Humanities Act, 20 U.S.C. §951(5).

2. James Broughton, *Seeing the Light* (City Lights, 1977), p. 13.

3. James Douglas in the May 1922 *Sunday Express*, quoted in Edward de Grazia's *Girls Lean Back Everywhere*, p. 26.

4. The incident is recalled in Livingston Biddle, *Our Government and the Arts* (American Council on the Arts, 1988), p. 316.

5. Letters of January 25 and February 2, 1984, reprinted in *Hearing on the Grant Making Process of the National Endowment for the Arts Before the Subcommittee on Postsecondary Education, House Committee on Education and Labor*, June 28, 1984; see also William Farrell and Warren Weaver, Jr., "Briefing," *New York Times*, Feb. 23, 1984, p. 14.

6. Ibid.

7. Statement to the Senate Subcommittee on Education, March 29, 1990, reprinted in Richard Bolton, ed., *Culture Wars*, pp. 159–60.

8. John E. Frohnmayer, "A Litany of Taboo," *Kansas Journal of Law and Public Policy*, Spring 1992, p. 48.

9. Ibid.

10. Carole S. Vance, "Reagan's Revenge: Restructuring the NEA," *Art in America*, Nov. 1990, p. 55.

11. Lucy Lippard, "Andres Serrano: The Spirit and the Letter," *Art in America*, April 1990, p. 242.

12. Senator Patrick Leahy made this point during a 1989 Senate debate: see Bolton, *Culture Wars*, p. 4.

13. Quoted in the *Newsletter on Intellectual Freedom* of the American Library Association, July 1992, p. 126.

14. Beverly Mabry, "Library Controversy Sparked," *Carroll County Times*, June 20, 1992, p. A13.

15. *Keyishian* v. *Board of Regents*, 385 U.S. 589, 603 (1967).

16. Marcelle Clements, "Karen Finley's Rage, Love, Hate, and Hope," *New York Times*, July 22, 1990, p. 5.

17. Margaret Mifflin, "Performance Art," *ARTnews*, April 1992, p. 86.

18. Patti Hartigan, "Playwright Gives Galleries His Grant to Protest NEA," *Boston Globe*, June 3, 1992, pp. 41, 43.

Chapter 7

1. See Walter Kendrick, *The Secret Museum: Pornography in Modern Culture* (Viking Penguin, 1987), pp. 11–13.

2. Webster's New World Dictionary of the American Language (College ed. 1957), p. 1138.

3. *Cohen* v. *California*, 403 U.S. 15, 25 (1971).

4. Natalie Anger, "This Can't Be Love," *New York Times Book Review*, Nov. 29, 1992, p. 7.

5. See Patricia M. Robinson, "The Historical Repression of Women's Sexuality," in Carole S. Vance, ed., *Pleasure and Danger* (Routledge and Keegan Paul, 1984), p. 255.

6. Casey Finch, "Two of a Kind," *Artforum*, Feb. 1992, p. 90.

7. See Jessica Benjamin, "Master and Slave: The Fantasy of Erotic Domination," in Ann Snitow, Christine Stansell, and Sharon Thompson, eds., *Powers of Desire: The Politics of Sexuality* (Monthly Review Press, 1983), p. 280.

8. See David Steinberg, "The Roots of Pornography," in Michael S. Kimmel, ed., *Men Confront Pornography* (Meridian, 1990), p. 56.

9. Finch, "Two of a Kind," *Artforum*, Feb. 1992, p. 90.

10. Steinberg, "The Roots of Pornography," in *Men Confront Pornography*, p. 57.

11. See Bernie Zilbergeld, "Pornography as Therapy," in *Men Confront Pornography*, p. 120; Patricia Gillan, "Therapeutic Uses of Obscenity," and H. J. Eysenck, "Psychology and Obscenity," in Rajeev Dhavan and Christie Davies, eds., *Censorship and Obscenity* (Rowman and Littlefield, 1978).

12. Letter from Patti Britton, Ph.D., to Senator Patrick Leahy, opposing the proposed "Pornography Victims Compensation Act," Feb. 10, 1992.

13. According to *Adult Video News*, cited in Wendy Melillo, "Can Pornography Lead to Violence?" *Washington Post*, July 21, 1992, p. 10.

14. See de Grazia, *Girls Lean Back Everywhere*, pp. 540–46.

15. Steinberg, "The Roots of Pornography," in *Men Confront Pornography*, p. 57.

16. Faye Ginsburg, "The Body Politic: The Defense of Sexual Restriction by Anti-Abortion Activists," in Carole S. Vance, ed., *Pleasure and Danger*, p. 173.

17. *The Report of the Commission on Obscenity and Pornography* (the

"Lockhart Report") (Bantam ed., 1970), p. 53.

18. American Civil Liberties Union Public Policy Report, *Polluting the Censorship Debate: A Summary and Critique of the Final Report of the Attorney General's Commission on Pornography* (1986), p. 43, citing Transcript of Proceedings, U.S. Department of Justice, Attorney General's Commission on Pornography, May 2, 1986.

19. Marcia Pally, *Sense and Censorship: The Vanity of Bonfires*, vol. 1, (Americans for Constitutional Freedom, 1991), p. 22, quoting *New York Times*, May 17, 1986. See also the response of three leading researchers to the Meese Commission in Daniel Linz, Steven Penrod and Edward Donnerstein, "The Attorney General's Commission on Pornography: the Gap Between 'Findings' and 'Facts,'" *American Bar Foundation Research Journal* (1987), p. 713.

20. In sworn deposition testimony in a lawsuit brought against the Department of Justice challenging its tactics (*PHE, Inc.* v. *Department of Justice*).

21. See, for example, Patricia Gillan, "Therapeutic Uses of Obscenity," and H. J. Eysenck, "Psychology and Obscenity," in *Censorship and Obscenity*, pp. 127, 148, and the extensive sources cited in these articles.

22. H. J. Eysenck, "Psychology and Obscenity," in *Censorship and Obscenity*, pp. 163–64.

23. See Gillan, "Therapeutic Uses of Obscenity," in *Censorship and Obscenity* p. 145; Marcia Pally, *Sense and Censorship*, vol. 2, p. 61.

24. Pally, *Sense and Censorship*, vol. 2, pp. 48–49.

25. There's an extensive literature summarizing the many studies that have been done about both correlation and causation; a good bibliography is in volume 2 of Pally's *Sense and Censorship*.

26. Ibid., vol. 2, pp. 39–40.

27. Linz, Penrod, and Donnerstein, "The Attorney General's Commission on Pornography," in *American Bar Foundation Research Journal* (1987), p. 714.

28. See Edward Donnerstein and Daniel Linz, "Mass Media, Sexual Violence, and Male Viewers: Current Theory and Research," in *Men Confront Pornography*, p. 228.

29. Home Office, *Report of the Committee on Obscenity and Film Censorship* (1979), pp. 86–87, quoted in Gordon Hawkins and Franklin Zimring, *Pornography in a Free Society* (Cambridge University Press, 1988), p. 117.

30. Fred Small, "Pornography and Censorship," in *Men Confront Pornography*, pp. 74–75.

31. Robin Morgan, in "Theory and Practice: Pornography and Rape," reprinted in Robin Morgan, *The Word of a Woman: Feminist Dispatches 1968–1992* (Norton, 1992), p. 88.

32. British author Suzanne Moore, quoted in letter from Leanne Katz to the *New York Times Book Review*, Aug. 30, 1992, p. 15.

33. Catharine MacKinnon, *Feminism Unmodified* (Harvard University Press, 1987), pp. 130, 154, 171–72.

34. Andrea Dworkin, *Pornography: Men Possessing Women* (Penguin, 1979), p. 23.

35. See *Feminism Unmodified*, pp. 143, 144–45, 261.

36. Hawkins and Zimring, *Pornography in a Free Society*, p. 163.

37. The term is columnist Ellen Willis's; see *New York Newsday*, Feb. 25, 1992, p. 78.

38. Letter to *Harper's* magazine, May 1992, p. 4.

39. Morgan, *The Word of a Woman*, p. 85.

Chapter 8

1. Lucy Lippard, "Andres Serrano: The Spirit and the Letter," *Art in America*, April 1990, p. 239.

2. Reported in *Variety*, Aug. 10, 1988.

3. Reported in *Variety*, Sept. 7, 1988.

4. David Thompson and Ian Christie, eds., *Scorsese on Scorsese* (Faber and Faber, 1989) p. xxii.

5. *Joseph Burstyn, Inc.* v. *Wilson*, 343 U.S. 495, 504–5 (1952).

6. See Patti Hartigan, "Boston's Culture Shock," *Boston Globe*, July 29, 1990, p. 12.

7. See Carmilly-Weinberger, *Fear of Art: Censorship and Freedom of Expression in Art*, p. 18; Richard Cocke, *Veronese* (Jupiter Books, 1980), pp. 16, 79. H. W. Janson, in his *History of Art* (Abrams, 1962) p. 382, notes that although the inquisitors thought the painting represented the Last Supper, Veronese never made it clear what he intended.

8. See Clapp, *Art Censorship: A Chronology of Proscribed and Prescribed Art*, pp. 224–26.

9. Letter from Tolstoy to the manager of the Imperial Moscow Theatres, 1892, quoted in Aylmer Maude, *The Life of Tolstoy* (Oxford, 1987), vol. 2, p. 266.

10. Rebecca Zurier, *Art for the Masses: A Radical Magazine and Its Graphics* (Temple University Press, 1988), p. 61.

11. Two Supreme Court decisions established these basic rules: *New York Times* v. *Sullivan*, 376 U.S. 254 (1964), and *Brandenburg* v. *Ohio*, 395 U.S. 444 (1969).

12. Larry Ellison, president of the Massachusetts Association of Minority Law Enforcement Officers, quoted in the *Boston Herald,* August 6, 1992, p. 43.

13. Gerald Levin, "Why We Won't Withdraw 'Cop Killer,'" *Wall Street Journal,* June 24, 1992, p. 20.

14. "Rock Clips," *Village Voice,* Sept. 22, 1992, p. 86.

15. Jon Pareles, "The Disappearance of Ice-T's 'Cop Killer,'" *New York Times,* July 30, 1992, p. C13.

16. Luther Campbell and John R. Miller, *As Nasty as They Wanna Be: The Uncensored Story of Luther Campbell of the 2 Live Crew* (Barricade Books, 1992), p. 184.

17. Richard Harrington, "The FBI as Music Critic: Letter on Rap Record Seen as Intimidation," *Washington Post,* Oct. 4, 1989, p. B7.

18. American Library Association, *Newsletter on Intellectual Freedom,* July 1992, p. 124.

19. Delfattore, *What Johnny Shouldn't Read,* p. 109, quoting interview with Bay County, Florida, School Superintendent Leonard Hall in the *Panama City News Herald,* June 11, 1987.

20. Quoted in the *Newsletter on Intellectual Freedom,* July 1992, p. 117.

21. See Stephanie Barron, ed., *"Degenerate Art": The Fate of the Avant-Garde in Nazi Germany,* (Los Angeles County Museum of Art, 1991).

Conclusion

1. 1990 anti-censorship film produced by the Michigan Intellectual Freedom Coalition.

2. Clarke Blacker, guitarist for the Dallas punk rock group Stick Men With Ray Guns, quoted in McNear, "It's Only Rock 'n' Roll," *Dallas Observer,* Sept. 12, 1985.

3. Frank Rich, "Discovering Family Values at 'Falsettos,'" *New York Times,* July 12, 1992, Arts and Leisure sec., p. 1.

4. Robin Wright, "A Reporter at Large: A Teheran Spring," *The New Yorker,* June 22, 1992.

Afterword

1. *Whitney v. California,* 274 U.S. 357, 377 (1927) (concurring opinion).

A FEW SUGGESTIONS
FOR FURTHER READING

〰〰〰〰〰〰〰〰〰〰〰〰〰〰〰〰〰〰〰〰〰〰〰〰

Censorship in General

Richard Bolton, ed., *Culture Wars: Documents from the Recent Controversies in the Arts* (The New Press 1992).

Stephanie Barron, ed., *"Degenerate Art": The Fate of the Avant-Garde in Nazi Germany* (Los Angeles County Museum of Art 1991).

Jane Clapp, *Art Censorship: A Chronology of Proscribed and Prescribed Art* (Scarecrow Press 1972).

Edward de Grazia, *Girls Lean Back Everywhere: The Law of Obscenity and the Assault on Genius* (Random House 1992).

Joan Delfattore, *What Johnny Shouldn't Read—Textbook Censorship in America* (Yale University Press 1992).

Donna Demac, *Liberty Denied: The Current Rise of Censorship in America* (Rutgers University Press 1990).

Stephen Dubin, *Arresting Images: Impolitic Art and Uncivil Actions* (Routledge 1992).

Ira Glasser, *Visions of Liberty* (Arcade 1991).

Walter Kendrick, *The Secret Museum: Pornography in Modern Culture* (Viking 1987).

Dave Marsh, *50 Ways to Fight Censorship* (Thunder's Mouth Press 1991).

New York Public Library, *Censorship: 500 Years of Conflict* (1984).

Kenneth Norwick, and Jerry Chasen, *The Rights of Authors, Artists, and Other Creative People* (ACLU/Southern Illinois. University Press 1992).

Charles Rembar, *The End of Obscenity* (Simon and Schuster 1968).

Samuel Walker, *In Defense of American Liberties: A History of the ACLU* (Oxford University Press 1990).

Moshe Carmilly-Weinberger, *Fear of Art: Censorship and Freedom of Expression in Art* (Bowker 1986).

Art & Sexuality

The Body in Question (Melissa Harris, ed., Aperture 1990).
Edward Lucie-Smith, *Sexuality in Western Art* (Thames and Hudson 1991).
Pleasure and Danger (Carole S. Vance, ed., Routledge and Keegan Paul 1984).
Powers of Desire: The Politics of Sexuality (Ann Snitow, Christine Stansell, and Sharon Thompson, eds., Monthly Review Press 1983).

Pornography

Censorship and Obscenity (Rajeev Dhavan, and Christie Davies, eds., Rowman and Littlefield 1978).
Andrea Dworkin, *Pornography: Men Possessing Women* (Plume/Penguin 1981).
Gordon Hawkins and Franklin Zimring, *Pornography in a Free Society* (Cambridge University Press 1988).
Catharine MacKinnon, *Feminism Unmodified* (Harvard University Press 1987).
Men Confront Pornography (Michael Kimmel, ed., Meridian 1990).
Marcia Pally, *Sense and Censorship: The Vanity of Bonfires* (Americans for Constitutional Freedom 1991).
Pornography and Sexual Aggression (Neil Malamuth and Edward Donnerstein, eds., Academic Press 1984).
The Report of the Commission on Obscenity and Pornography (William B. Lockhard, chairman, Bantam 1970).
U.S. Department of Justice, *Final Report of the Attorney General's Commission on Pornography* (1986) (2 vols.).

Movie Censorship & Blacklisting

David Caute, *The Great Fear* (Simon and Schuster 1978).
Larry Ceplar and Steven Englund, *The Inquisition in Hollywood* (Anchor 1980).
Leonard Leff and Jerold Simmons, *The Dame in the Kimono: Hollywood, Censorship, and Production Code from the 1920s to the 1960s* (Anchor 1990).
Merle Miller, *The Judges and the Judged* (Doubleday 1952).
Victor Navasky, *Naming Names* (Penguin 1980).

INDEX